Beethoven
for KIDS

His Life and Music

WITH 21 ACTIVITIES

Helen Bauer

CHICAGO
REVIEW
PRESS

Library of Congress Cataloging-in-Publication Data

Bauer, Helen, 1943-

    Beethoven for kids : his life and music with 21 activities / Helen Bauer.

        p. cm. — (For kids series)

    Includes bibliographical references and index.

    ISBN 978-1-56976-711-5 (pbk.)

    1. Beethoven, Ludwig van, 1770-1827—Juvenile literature.   2. Composers—

Austria—Biography—Juvenile literature.   I. Title. II. Series.

    ML3930.B4B38 2011

    780.92—dc22

    [B]

                                             2011018131

Cover and interior design: Monica Baziuk

Interior illustrations: Mark Baziuk

Cover images: Beethoven, New York Public Library; Beethoven's home,

Ira F. Brilliant Center for Beethoven Studies; Napoleon Stamp, Dreamstime;

Burgtheater in Vienna, Library of Congress; Fortepiano, Paul McNulty.

Copyright © 2011 by Helen Bauer

All rights reserved

First edition

Published by Chicago Review Press, Incorporated

814 North Franklin Street

Chicago, Illinois 60610

ISBN 978-1-56976-711-5

Printed in the United States of America

5   4   3   2

Dedicated to Edward Bauer—for all the years.

CONTENTS

NOTE TO READERS

*L*UDWIG VAN BEETHOVEN created amazing music, and his genius and talent had a tremendous influence on future classical composers. Beethoven's creations are studied and dissected by scholars and in music classes. His compositions are performed by student orchestras and choruses throughout the world. His significance and fame in the world of classical music are immeasurable. It is impossible to separate Beethoven's life from the world and language of music; in this book I have attempted to explore and interweave the two so that they illuminate each other.

Important musical terms appear in bold type when they are first introduced in the book and are further defined in the glossary at the back. In addition, "Music Notes" sidebars throughout the book delve into some of these concepts more deeply. It is my hope that young readers, at all levels of music knowledge or experience, will come away with not only a better understanding of Beethoven the man but also his musical accomplishments and the ideas that he believed in and followed throughout his lifetime.

♣ Beethoven's grave monument. Photograph by Daderot

INTRODUCTION

"I am resolved to rise superior to every obstacle."
—LUDWIG VAN BEETHOVEN, from a letter dated June 1, 1801

CAN YOU IMAGINE needing and wanting to listen to something you cannot hear? Is it possible for someone who cannot hear to compose music? How would a deaf composer cope with such a handicap? How would it affect his life? Would his music be appreciated by those who listened to it? Can a deaf composer make an impact on the world?

Ludwig van Beethoven faced and overcame many obstacles in his lifetime. Early on he had to deal with poverty, illness, and an alcoholic father. His unhappy childhood was filled with loneliness and fear. As a teenager he realized that he had to take on the responsibility of supporting his mother and younger siblings. He also began to suffer from poor health that would plague him for the remainder of his life.

Ludwig van Beethoven. *Library of Congress LC-USZ62-13745*

Living in a time of upheaval, revolution, and change in European society greatly influenced Beethoven's thoughts. He forced himself onto the musical stage, employing his enormous talents and strong personality. His music provided him with an entrance into the great palaces and concert halls of the era; his ideals and character caused him to stand up for his own rights and the civil liberties of all mankind.

Beethoven was 27 years old when he began to lose his hearing. In Beethoven's day there were no technological solutions and no effective medical treatments for his hearing loss. Sign language was just starting to be developed and was not yet an established method of communication for the deaf. Amplifying cones called "ear trumpets" were available, but they were of limited use. Beethoven used ear trumpets to assist him until he was completely deaf and the ear trumpets could no longer transmit any sounds to his ear. However, he was able to sense the vibrations of his instruments as he played them, which he found to be helpful. But nothing the composer tried was able to reverse, halt the progress of, or even manage his condition.

Beethoven was, from an early age onward, a difficult and complex person with a very intense personality. Scholars attribute some of his behavior to his hearing loss, a process that worsened over a 20-year period. His hearing loss added to his insecurities and fears, especially during the

many years he spent trying to hide the fact that he was having trouble hearing sounds. Beethoven's sense about what was right and his high moral ideals dictated many of his actions. Social situations were uncomfortable for Beethoven, although he liked being with people. In addition, he had a hard time with the exaggerated elegant manners of his day.

Beethoven spent many years trying to keep his friends and audiences from learning that he was suffering from many physical ailments in addition to his increasing deafness. This concealment often made his actions appear odd and unusual to those who had no knowledge of his medical condition. Once his hearing loss was complete, Beethoven withdrew from most social settings. This increased his feeling of isolation and caused him to be suspicious and distrustful.

Being deaf makes it hard to communicate with others. Helen Keller, who lost both her hearing and her sight, stated that blindness separates people from things but deafness separates people from people. Beethoven lost more than his hearing—he lost his ability to connect to other people. Yet this disability may have actually helped Beethoven as a composer, because he had to be able to hear the music he created inside himself without the distractions of the outside world.

Beethoven's works are true masterpieces; many of his pieces were groundbreaking and set the standards for all to follow. He was a fantastic architect of music, always seeking perfection. Some of his greatest music shocked and surprised the audiences of his day. The works were far too complex and forward-thinking for 19th-century listeners, musicians, and critics to fully understand. Beethoven understood this fact and stated that these works "are not for you, but for a later age." His creations continue to inspire and uplift people all over the world. This is a true story about one of the most famous composers of all time, one who overcame many obstacles that caused him pain and suffering but could not stop him.

TIME LINE

1770 ∞ Ludwig van Beethoven is baptized on December 17 in Bonn; born to Johann van Beethoven and Maria Magdalena Keverich

1774 ∞ Brother Caspar Carl baptized

1776 ∞ Brother Nikolaus Johann baptized

1778 ∞ Beethoven's first concert, March 26

1780 ∞ Beethoven becomes a pupil of Christian Gottlob Neefe, organist at the Court of Bonn and director of the National Theater

1783 ∞ Variations on Dressler's March in C Minor is published

1787 ∞ Ludwig travels to Vienna and meets Mozart
Maria Magdalena van Beethoven, Ludwig's mother, dies on July 17

1789 ∞ The storming of Bastille in Paris
Beethoven supports his family; becomes a violist in the court orchestra

1790 ∞ Beethoven composes Cantata on the Death of the Emperor Joseph II

1791 ∞ Mozart dies on December 5
Beethoven becomes a music teacher for the von Breuning family

1792 ∞ Beethoven leaves Bonn for Vienna
Johann van Beethoven, Ludwig's father, dies

1793 ∞ Beethoven studies with Haydn

1796 ∞ Symptoms of deafness begin
Beethoven travels to Leipzig, Prague, Dresden, and Berlin

1798 ∞ Beethoven composes the Piano Sonata in C Minor (*Pathétique* Sonata) (op. 13)

1799 ∞ Napoléon becomes first consul of the new French government

1800 ∞ Beethoven conducts his First Symphony

1802 ∞ Beethoven writes the Heiligenstadt Testament and composes Symphony no. 2 (op. 36)

1804 ∞ Napoléon crowns himself emperor; the Napoleonic Wars begin

1805 ∞ First public performance of *Fidelio*

Vibrating Sounds

"Then let us all do what is right, strive with all our might toward the unattainable, develop as fully as we can the gifts God has given us, and never stop learning."
—Ludwig van Beethoven

O N A COLD day in December 1770 Ludwig van Beethoven was born. White snow covered the rooftop above the tiny attic room where his mother was now resting after his birth. All was still outside except for the wind swirling the layers of snow into soft hills, and yet the world surrounding this new baby was rapidly changing.

In the part of Europe then called the Holy Roman Empire was the town of Bonn (today a thriving city in Germany), where the family lived on a street called Bonngasse (Bonn Lane). They rented rooms in the garden wing of the house. The chilled air of Europe was vibrating with new, exciting sounds. Outside the parlor window, people were talking

✦ The town of Bonn in 1700.

about gaining freedom from tyrannical rulers and monarchs in Europe and in lands far away. From the back of the house, the sounds of music, its harmonies and **rhythms**, pulsed from the small rooms.

Baby Ludwig's father, Johann, and his grandfather, also named Ludwig, were musicians in the court of the elector of Cologne. The elector was the archbishop placed in charge of the territory by the emperor Joseph II. Grandfather Ludwig had come to Bonn from Belgium many years before. Now Ludwig's only son was a singer in the same court. Johann also gave music lessons to the children of wealthy aristocrats. These few students brought in some additional money to help support Johann's wife, Maria Magdalena, and their new baby. Maria Magdalena had been a young widow when Johann married her in 1767, just a few days before her 21st birthday. She had lost her first husband and an infant son.

Even with the extra income from his students, Johann did not earn much, but Grandfather Ludwig often helped them, especially after his new namesake, Ludwig, was born and survived. This Ludwig was actually the second child to which the couple had given that name. Their first son had been baptized Ludwig Maria one year before but had passed away when he was only six

🎵 The house where Beethoven was born, now the Beethoven Museum, Bonn. Photograph by Sir James

days old. His parents and grandfather hoped and prayed that this new Ludwig would be strong and well enough to reach adulthood.

Being born into a family of musicians does not always guarantee musical talent, but in this case the youngster was clearly very musically gifted. When Ludwig was three years old, Johann began to teach him to play the violin as well as a stringed keyboard instrument called the **harpsichord**. Ludwig was so small he had to stand on a wooden bench to reach the keyboard. Johann noted that his son learned quickly—he seemed to breathe in the music.

Maria Magdalena was a gentle, kind, and patient woman, but her husband was harsh and demanding. Johann had a terrible temper and spent a lot of his time in the local taverns, often coming home drunk and in a foul mood. He would make little Ludwig practice for hours and even wake him up late at night for a lesson. Johann was aware that about 15 years earlier a six-year-old musical genius named Wolfgang Amadeus Mozart, who was considered a child prodigy (an unusually talented child), had earned a lot of money by performing all over Europe. Johann was sure that his son was just as gifted. He was hoping to make money in the same way from his son's talent, so he pushed Ludwig very hard. Even though his father was critical and forced him to practice, young Ludwig loved music.

The Industrial Revolution

The Industrial Revolution began in the United Kingdom in the 1700s and soon spread to the rest of Europe, North America, and the world, introducing steam-powered machines for producing and transporting products. As technology advanced, the Western world moved from a household economy to an industry-based economy.

The Scottish inventor James Watt made changes to Thomas Newcomen's steam engine that led to the development of the steam locomotive and the steamboat as well as more powerful factory machinery. Watt's improvements not only increased the power of the steam engine but made it more reliable. The steam engine replaced people and animals as the energy source for the Industrial Revolution. It drove the machines of the mills and factories and allowed the mass production of goods.

New inventions also mechanized farming. In 1788 the Scotsman Andrew Meikle patented his invention, the threshing machine, which separated grain from its stalks. Fewer people were needed to harvest crops as machines took over human labor. People who had been spending their lives farming now moved to cities and took jobs in factories. The Industrial Revolution changed an agricultural society into a city-centered economy.

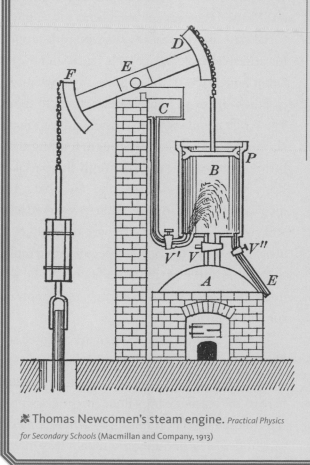

❦ Thomas Newcomen's steam engine. *Practical Physics for Secondary Schools* (Macmillan and Company, 1913)

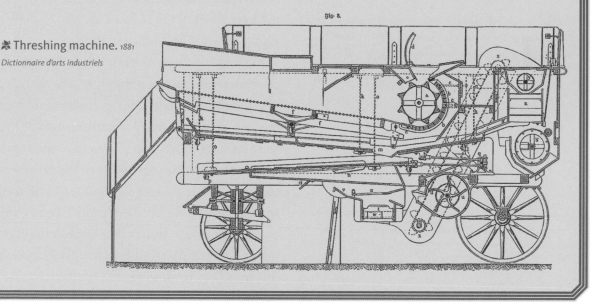

❦ Threshing machine. *1881*
Dictionnaire d'arts industriels

🎵 Beethoven's grandfather, also named Ludwig van Beethoven. Reproduced with the permission of the Ira F. Brilliant Center for Beethoven Studies, San José State University

Grandfather Ludwig passed away when his grandson was three years old; young Ludwig's musical talent was a great comfort in the years following his adored grandfather's death. The child always kept a small portrait of his grandfather, who had also been his godfather, close by. The artist Leopold Radoux had depicted a serious but kindly looking man in a fur-trimmed jacket and velvet robe pointing to a musical **score**. Even though Beethoven would move many times in the years to come, this cherished portrait always moved with him.

The Beethoven family was growing. Several more children were born, but only two boys, Nikolaus Johann and Caspar Carl, survived past infancy. Needing additional space, the family moved many times. They often found lodgings in the lower part of town near the river, in the less expensive areas of Bonn.

During Beethoven's childhood, the society, economy, and politics of Europe were changing. The ancient social traditions and political arrangements that had ruled and organized people's lives were starting to fall apart. Even in a small town like Bonn, the chimney stacks of factories were rising as power machinery replaced hand tools and manufacturing replaced farming. People who had lived in the countryside began moving to towns. Cities grew steadily as people found jobs there, and a new working class was forming. Ruling monarchies feared they would be overthrown by the common people as a revolutionary mood flooded the continent.

Learning About the World

WHEN LUDWIG was six years old he entered the local primary school. He began learning about the world outside of his home. Ludwig understood that he had been born into a lower social class than the aristocrats who rode around town in splendid carriages. He had seen how his father bowed low to the nobility and how he was careful to be extra polite when talking to them. These rich people wore beautiful and well-made clothes. The aristocratic women, holding their little dogs, would stroll through the parks of Bonn in their lovely dresses and fancy hats. The men were clad in elaborate, white-powdered wigs and colorful silk jackets. The vast differences in lifestyle between the rich and poor seemed unfair to the little boy. Even at such a young age he was not impressed by status that was based simply on someone's birth.

Ludwig did not seem to learn much in school. He was not good with numbers, had a hard time with spelling, and his handwriting was impossible to read, the teacher complained. In the classroom the children used hornbooks, which were pieces of wood with a handle on which a lesson was attached then covered with a thin piece of horn

Make a Hornbook and Quill Pen

IN BEETHOVEN'S time there were no blackboards in classrooms, and books were expensive. Children learned how to read using hornbooks. To keep the lessons clean, a thin piece of translucent animal horn was placed over the paper. A hole in the handle allowed the hornbook to be tied to the child's belt. Quill pens, made out of large bird feathers, were used for centuries as writing instruments until they were replaced by dip pens with wooden holders. You can make a hornbook to display a poem or short story that you enjoy.

You'll Need

∾ Stiff piece of cardboard, 9 by 11 inches
∾ Scissors
∾ Goose or turkey feather from a craft store
∾ Bottle of dark-colored ink
∾ Scrap paper
∾ Poem or short story you like or write
∾ Paper, 7 by 9 inches
∾ Clear plastic sheet or waxed paper, 7½ by 9½ inches
∾ Glue stick or thumbtacks
∾ Hole punch
∾ 10 inches of yarn or string

1. Draw a paddle shape on the cardboard to measure 8 by 10 inches, and cut it out.

2. Make your quill pen by snipping the tip of the feather quill into a V shape with scissors.

3. Dip the end of the quill pen into the ink and practice writing with it on scrap paper. It may take some time before you are satisfied with your ability to work with the quill.

4. Write or copy the poem or short story on the 7-by-9-inch paper using the quill.

5. Attach the paper to the cardboard with glue, centering the paper on the cardboard.

6. Cover the paper with the plastic sheet or waxed paper. Glue or thumbtack the edges to the cardboard.

7. Have an adult punch a hole in the handle. Loop the yarn or string through the hole and tie the ends together to create a loop to wear around your wrist.

to keep the page clean. Ludwig's hornbook was always messy, and the paper containing his lesson was often torn and blurry.

Ludwig did not make many friends at school. Some of the children were cruel to him and made fun of his shabby, unwashed clothes or the fact that his hands and face always appeared to be dirty. After being teased and taunted several times, Ludwig tried to avoid his classmates. His mother suggested that the other children would be nicer to him if he would smile at them more often, but the boy did not think that a silly grin was a good reply to the ridicule of his classmates. Instead of smiling Ludwig sternly responded that when he

The Patronage System

For centuries in Europe the wealthy and powerful controlled the arts. All artists, writers, and musicians were hired and supported by men who had authority either as rulers of the people or as high-ranking members of the clergy. Some royal and noble women were active patrons as well. This system was known as the patronage system. A patron could choose which artists to support and tell them what to produce. This severely limited the artists' freedom to create. They were considered servants of their patrons and were expected to try to please their patrons' tastes and demands. These wealthy and powerful sponsors often used the arts to glorify their own social or political ambitions.

Great works of art and music were often crafted under this system, even if the works weren't of the artist's choosing. Michelangelo preferred to carve marble sculptures when he was commissioned by the pope to paint the Sistine Chapel ceiling. The artist wanted to turn down this project. Realizing that his future income was at stake, Michelangelo gave the world a fabulous work of art.

Beethoven is credited as the first composer to have avoided complete dependence on the patronage system. By the time his music was well known, the middle class could afford to attend concerts and purchase his scores. Still, he did rely on patrons for much of his income. Patrons often commissioned Beethoven for projects, but because he had other sources of income he had the freedom to say no.

❧ "Miss Campion" holding a hornbook. *History of the Horn-Book* by Andrew Tuer, 1661

became a famous musician no one would care about his clothes or dare to treat him badly.

When Ludwig came home from school he spent many hours practicing the violin and the harpsichord. He loved the feel of the instruments and the beautiful sounds they could make. Music made the rest of the day feel cheerful and wonderful. He especially liked to take a **theme** written by another composer and change it. Many ideas came into his mind about how a short tune, called a **motif**, could be varied and altered. His amazing talent for **improvisation** was astonishing for someone so young.

Needing to practice his instruments, Ludwig usually had very little time to play with other children. He must have been able to hear other youngsters in the courtyard playing their favorite games, such as Blind and Bell. His younger brothers, Caspar Carl and Nikolaus Johann, were free to run outside to join in. Music was Ludwig's playmate.

Dreams of Fame

IN MARCH 1778 Johann decided that his son was ready to give a concert and earn a reputation as a child prodigy just like Mozart. There was much money to be made and a fruitful career to build. Johann had the future all planned out when he made the arrangements for a public concert to be

---

Music Notes: What Is Improvisation?

Improvisation is a technique that alters the **melody** but allows the listener to still recognize the original tune. A skillful musician uses imagination and inventive ideas to improvise. From about 1600 and continuing for almost 300 years, musicians were expected to be able to improvise. Early scores left much up to the performers, since music was not always composed for a specific instrument and the performers were expected to embellish, or add to, the work.

The talent of improvisation was highly prized during the early periods of Western classical music and is an ability that is valued in jazz musicians today. At the beginning of the 1900s composers no longer wanted musicians to alter their music, and improvisation went out of style. Today many experimental composers write pieces that allow or require improvisation.

Musicians can select from many techniques for improvising a melody; they may make minor changes or apply a high degree of **variation** to a theme. The choices range from simple **ornamentation**—decorating the **notes** with **embellishments** such as grace notes, which are quickly played notes that are not written into the original score, while keeping the notes in the same order in which they are originally presented—to a complete alteration of the original theme. Improvisation is composing while playing; it showcases originality and the ability to be creative either as a soloist or as a performer within a group. Composers Johann Sebastian Bach, Mozart, Beethoven, and Franz Liszt were masters of this art.

---

held in the city of Cologne, 15 miles away. Father and son traveled by stagecoach to the boy's first public performance. Johann was in a joyful mood sitting inside the coach chatting with the other passengers. He even joined in with the others singing German folk songs. Entering the

Play Blind and Bell

BLIND AND Bell was a favorite game of German children in the 1700s.

You'll Need

∞ 6 or more players

∞ Cloth, such as a bandana or scarf, to use as a blindfold

∞ Bell

1. Six or more players sit in a circle facing the center.

2. Select someone to be the game leader and one to be blindfolded.

3. The game leader blindfolds the chosen player and spins him or her around three times in the center of the circle.

4. The game leader joins the circle and passes the bell to another player. The players pass it around the circle a few times.

5. The game leader points at the person who should ring the bell, and that person rings it.

6. The blindfolded person guesses who is holding the bell.

7. If the blindfolded player is right, the bell holder becomes the person blindfolded in the next round. If the blindfolded player is wrong, he or she keeps trying until correctly naming the person holding the bell.

city, one of the passengers pointed out the sights. Ludwig was amazed by what he saw; Cologne was much larger than Bonn. The city touched the edges of the wide Rhine River, so many boats and barges passed by as the horses trotted down the cobblestoned riverbank road. On the way to their lodgings the passengers rode by the huge Cologne Cathedral and many impressive stone buildings decorated with elegant ornaments.

Although Ludwig was seven years old, his father had told the printer of the concert announcements that his son was only six. The flyers were posted all over Cologne, attracting many people to the performance. Johann thought this "little lie" would ensure that Ludwig would be noticed by important people at the concert and would become a star performer all over Europe. Due to his father's lie, Beethoven was never certain of his age. Even years later, when he obtained a copy of a certificate that plainly displayed December 17, 1770, as the date of his baptism, he still doubted that the date was accurate. He told his friends, "There was a brother born before me, who was also named Ludwig . . . but who died."

The boy knew that he had to perform perfectly. Lots of people were in the audience waiting to hear his music. He could not let his father down. His small hands must have felt icy cold. His father urged him forward. Calming himself, Ludwig walked to the center of the stage and began to play.

Before the emergence of railway systems and automobiles, people often journeyed by horse-drawn stagecoaches, which traveled fixed routes between stations or stages. Dreamstime

Although he performed very well, Ludwig could sense that his father was not happy on the return trip to Bonn. Ludwig sat very still on the bench, sometimes lifting his head up slightly so that he could peer out of the smudged and grimy window. The day after the concert Johann was even more upset and very disappointed that his dream had not come true: Ludwig had not been hailed as a child prodigy by the important people who had come to hear him perform.

2

A New Teacher

*"Recommend virtue to your children; it alone, not
money, can make them happy. I speak from experience;
this was what upheld me in time of misery."*
—Ludwig van Beethoven, from his Heiligenstadt Testament

Johann soon realized that he could not continue teaching music to his son. Ludwig had progressed beyond his father. The local court organist and other musicians were asked to give the youngster lessons. Ludwig enjoyed their instruction, especially on the piano and the pipe organ. Christian Gottlob Neefe, a composer, court organist, and conductor, arrived in Bonn to work for the archbishop, the elector of Cologne, who ruled that part of the empire. Neefe was told about a very promising young musician. In 1781, Neefe became Ludwig's teacher.

♫ Christian Gottlob Neefe.
Beethoven Museum, Bonn

Three years after Neefe arrived in Bonn, the elector died, and Archduke Maximilian Franz became the new elector of Cologne. The archduke was the brother of Queen Marie Antoinette of France and the brother of Emperor Joseph II and Emperor Leopold II of the Holy Roman Empire. Maximilian Franz loved music, so Ludwig's teacher brought his pupil to the court to introduce him to the new elector. Neefe told Maximilian that he wanted this youngster to be employed as a substitute organist when the teacher was absent from Bonn. Neefe also convinced the elector that the boy should be appointed as the assistant organist in the court chapel. This gave

The Hapsburg Rulers

The Hapsburg (also known as Habsburg) dynasty was one of the most important monarchies in Europe. For centuries all of the rulers of the Holy Roman Empire were members of this noble family that originally came from Switzerland. Rudolph I, the first of 19 emperors from the Hapsburg family, ascended the throne in 1273, and Hapsburgs continued to rule for 600 years. By the 16th century the imperial title was hereditary, passed from one generation to the next, allowing the Hapsburg Empire to expand over most of continental Europe through military conquest and alliances arranged through marriage.

A body of princes, called "electors," selected the emperor, who was then installed by the pope. In the 16th century the dynasty split into two branches. One branch ruled the Spanish kingdom that included the Netherlands and Italy, while the other branch ruled the Holy Roman Empire that included the German-speaking countries and Hungary. The Hapsburg Empire began to crumble 300 years later: Italy and Germany were no longer in its control, and people in other lands were seeking freedom and wanting to form their own countries. In 1918, at the end of World War I, the Republic of Austria was established, and the Hapsburg rule was over.

✵ The Hapsburg crown. Dreamstime

✵ Archduke Maximilian Franz of Austria.

Ludwig the chance to play the organ at masses and court functions.

Neefe saw greatness in his pupil. He believed that Beethoven was "the second Mozart." Speaking to music publishers, Neefe always praised Ludwig and mentioned his extraordinary talent. He even convinced the editors of a German music magazine to publish a notice about the youngster, which called him "a boy of most promising talent" and noted, "He plays the clavier very skillfully and with power [and] reads at sight very well.... This young genius deserves a subsidy in order to enable him to travel. He will surely become a second Mozart if he continues as well as he has begun."

Ludwig had also begun to compose music. Neefe realized that his student's gift for writing music was as great as his ability to play instruments. His teacher wanted this student to be exposed to the wider world of music outside of Bonn.

First Composition

WITH NEEFE's help and encouragement, Beethoven's first composition, nine Variations on Dressler's March in C Minor, was published when he was 13 years old. Being published meant that

♣ Variations on Dressler's March in C Minor.

Sing Your Own Musical Variation

FOR YOUNG Beethoven's first composition he created nine variations of one tune. A variation changes some part of a musical theme. It can be simple or very elaborate. Try your hand at varying a familiar song by singing it in several different ways.

You'll Need

∞ Friend

∞ Internet access

∞ Tape recorder, if you want to tape your variations

First, sing "Twinkle, Twinkle, Little Star" the way it was written.

VARIATION 1: Sing the song changing the rhythm by holding a note for a longer time or a shorter time.

VARIATION 2: Change the **dynamics,** or the **volume,** of your singing. Sing louder or softer during various parts of the song.

VARIATION 3: Add some musical ornaments to decorate the original melody. An ornament may be adding a note to an existing note or a trill, which is a rapid alternation between two adjacent notes on a scale.

VARIATION 4: Have someone join you in singing the song.

VARIATION 5: Both of you sing the song as a round.

For more examples of variations, go online to YouTube and search for: Mozart: 12 Variations "Ah vous dirai-je, Maman." Note how Mozart used this French folk song as a basis for 12 variations.

Using what you have heard, how would you change your variations?

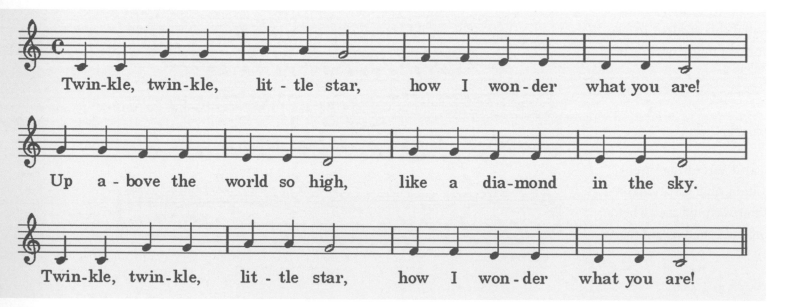

❧ "Twinkle, Twinkle, Little Star" Courtesy of Susan Silberman

Twin-kle, twin-kle, lit-tle star, how I won-der what you are!

Up a-bove the world so high, like a dia-mond in the sky.

Twin-kle, twin-kle, lit-tle star, how I won-der what you are!

people could purchase his music and perform it, and the young man was paid for this piece. It was probably composed in 1782, a year before it was printed by the publisher in 1783. The boy told his teacher that he believed a muse was whispering the ideas for his compositions into his ear.

The next year a set of three piano **sonatas**, musical pieces of several **movements**, followed the first composition. The young composer dedicated these sonatas to the elector. Ludwig had always liked the piano—he felt its power under his hands and saw its possibilities. His first works were written for this instrument. In his Variations on Dressler's March in C Minor the teenager took a fairly simple march and reinvented it. In each of the nine variations he kept the original melody but added new dimensions that made the melody sparkle and glimmer. The sonatas display his love for the piano, which was still being crafted into its final form many years after these pieces were written.

Now Ludwig's world was expanding to include composition, but his home life was becoming more difficult. By 1784 the Beethoven family was poorer than ever. Johann had either spent or wasted all the money he had inherited when his father had died 11 years earlier. Ludwig, as the oldest son, now had to help support the family. He earned barely enough from his published works and employment at court to feed and clothe his mother and brothers as well as himself.

Make a Silhouette Picture

BEFORE PHOTOGRAPHY was available, common people often had their image made into a silhouette, which is an outline of a person in profile. In the 1700s a silhouette cost far less than a painting or sculpture. The name of this art form comes from the French minister of finance, Étienne de Silhouette, who made it his hobby to cut these pictures while he was cutting back on spending in France.

You'll Need

∞ Large piece of white paper
∞ Tape
∞ Friend
∞ Chair
∞ Strong light source that can be aimed in a specific direction (a goose-necked lamp works well)
∞ Pencil
∞ Scissors
∞ White pencil
∞ 1 piece black construction paper
∞ 1 piece 8½-by-11-inch white construction paper
∞ Glue

1. Tape the large sheet of white paper to a wall.

2. Have your friend sit sideways and very still in a chair with the light source casting a shadow of your friend's profile onto the paper. Be sure to include part of the neck.

3. Adjust the light so that the profile fits on an 8½-by-11-inch piece of construction paper.

4. Stand so that your own shadow does not get in the way. Trace the outline of the shadow profile onto the paper with the pencil.

5. Remove the paper from the wall, and carefully cut out the profile with the scissors.

6. Trace the cutout onto the black construction paper with the white pencil. Cut out the silhouette.

7. Apply dabs of glue to the entire back of the silhouette and glue it onto the white construction paper. Wipe off any excess glue.

✷ Silhouette of Beethoven at 16.
Reproduced with the permission of the Ira F. Brilliant Center for Beethoven Studies, San José State University

15

The Age of Enlightenment

The 18th century is called the Age of Enlightenment because many thinkers and philosophers of that era sought to understand the world in a scientific and reasonable way. Just as scientists were developing methods of observing, investigating, and describing what they learned, philosophers wanted to use the same investigative and explanatory tools for understanding human beings' place in the universe. Enlightenment thinkers wrote, taught, and spoke out about political systems, religious beliefs, and artistic achievements. The availability of books and the ability of more people to read helped spread the ideas of these philosophers.

Thomas Paine, an Enlightenment thinker and one of the founding fathers of the United States, called this era the Age of Reason because scientific observation and facts overcame the ignorance and superstition of the past. The British philosopher John Locke believed that all people had "natural rights" and should be treated equally. Locke influenced many political philosophers and the founders of the United States. Thomas Jefferson used many of these ideas in the Declaration of Independence, which states that all men are endowed "with certain inalienable rights, and that among these are life, liberty and the pursuit of happiness."

The French philosopher Jean-Jacques Rousseau was another major thinker of the Enlightenment. His book *The Social Contract* (1762) explored the responsibilities of both the people and their governments. Rousseau argued that monarchs did not have a "divine right" to rule and that the people must establish a government that fairly sets the same laws and rules for all of its citizens.

Another French philosopher, François-Marie Arouet de Voltaire, was famous for his style and wit and went by the pen name Voltaire. He championed reason over superstition and promoted reforms of social, religious, economic, legal, and political institutions that would give people greater freedoms.

The Enlightenment caused many artists, including Beethoven, to rethink their creations and seek new ways to express themselves.

Voltaire at age 70. *Philosophical Dictionary* by François Voltaire, 1843

Making Friends

A MORE mature Ludwig was now making some friends. Franz Wegeler, a medical student, was one of them. Growing up in the same small town, they had known each other for some years before forming a friendship. Franz introduced Ludwig to a widow, Helene von Breuning. A cultured and kind lady, Frau von Breuning immediately liked the awkward teen. She hired Ludwig to teach two of her children the piano and often invited him to stay in her home. She sensed that he was uncomfortable around people and rather lonely, and she believed that his rough behavior cloaked a frightened and fragile boy. As Frau von Breuning explained to a friend, "It is our job to keep the insects off the flower."

The von Breuning family opened their home to the 14-year-old musician and made him feel welcome. Frau von Breuning had four children: Eleonore, Christoph, Stephan, and Lorenz. His friendship with Stephan lasted throughout Beethoven's life. The father of the von Breuning children had died, and their uncle, a teacher, lived with them. He taught the children about literature and engaged them in conversations about events all over the world. The atmosphere in the von Breuning house stimulated the young piano teacher's interest in culture and politics.

In the warm and friendly von Breuning home Ludwig could escape from the daily problems and turmoil of his own house. He could play their fine piano when his lessons with Eleonore and Lorenz were over. In this wealthy household Beethoven observed the gracious manners that the upper classes cherished. At their dinner table he had the opportunity to meet well-educated and cultured people, as well as many of Bonn's powerful aristocrats. From their discussions and conversations he learned about German literature, the Enlightenment, and popular ideas about government reform. In their library he especially liked to read the books of poetry; but even more, he enjoyed the dinnertime discussions and disputes about politics.

Franz Wegeler wrote that in the von Breuning's home Ludwig was "immediately treated like one of the family. He spent many days there, and many nights too." There was a stark contrast between his own household and this comfortable and happy place. In 1791, a letter Beethoven wrote to Frau von Breuning's daughter Eleonore proclaimed, "Never shall I forget you and your dear mother."

3

OPPORTUNITY AND UPHEAVAL

"He is no man; he is a devil. He will play me and all of us to death. And how he improvises!"
—THE MUSICIAN ABBÉ JOSEPH GELINEK, describing Beethoven

I N 1787, WHEN Ludwig was 17, Neefe felt that his pupil was ready to expand his musical education and his knowledge of the world. He spoke to the elector about paying Ludwig's expenses for a trip to the city of Vienna, a major cultural center of the German-speaking world. Maximilian agreed that this would be a great opportunity for the promising young man. Ludwig was thrilled at the prospect of seeing the city that he had heard so much about and was looking forward to meeting famous musicians. Neefe said that he would talk to Ludwig's Bonn patrons about providing new clothing and funds for other expenses. Count Ferdinand von Waldstein, one of these patrons, agreed to accompany the young composer to Vienna and to introduce him to Mozart.

Vienna was the capital of the Holy Roman Empire and Europe's musical capital. It was a lovely city that had wide main roads lined with beautiful, ornate buildings. On some street cor-ners musicians played their instruments while others presented puppet shows that entertained the passersby. The Danube River flowed through the city on its way to the Black Sea. There were parks with pathways, fountains, monuments, and statues. One of the largest parks, the Prater, had been given to the public by Emperor Joseph II. The upper classes enjoyed riding in their fancy carriages in the Prater. Many cafes and coffee-houses were located near the park. People would sit at the small tables on colorfully cushioned chairs and enjoy delicious Viennese pastries filled with whipped cream while sipping strong coffee, topped with fine flakes of chocolate, out of delicate china cups. Beethoven loved to walk in the Prater and through the streets surrounding the Hofburg Complex, the magnificent palaces of the Hapsburgs.

Meeting Mozart

Ludwig was happy to be in such a beautiful city. He was looking forward to his stay in Vienna as he unpacked the few belongings he had brought with him in a cloth satchel. While he put his clothes in the drawers, Ludwig might have pondered about how he wanted to impress Mozart so that perhaps he could become a pupil of this master musician and composer. Ludwig wanted his mother, whom he called Mutti, to be delighted by the

✤ The Danube River, Europe's second-longest river, flows along or through Germany, Austria, Slovakia, Hungary, Croatia, Serbia, Bulgaria, Romania, Ukraine, and Moldova. Library of Congress LC-DIG-ppmsc-09768

Mozart

Wolfgang Amadeus Mozart was born in Salzburg, Austria, in 1756. His father, Leopold, was a professional musician in the court orchestra and a music teacher. Mozart was playing the piano by ear when he was only three years old. By the age of six he was ready to perform for the Empress Maria Theresa. Mozart's father realized that his son had great talent and could earn a lot of money, so he arranged concert tours throughout Europe.

Young Mozart entertained audiences in many countries, and his reputation as a child prodigy grew. He could sight-read piano music easily and could improvise any given theme with skill. He could also play the violin and the viola. Leopold Mozart arranged for as many concerts as he could. Some days the child would perform for the court, at a private concert for the nobility, and at a public concert later in the day. Each performance lasted at least one and a half hours.

Mozart moved to Vienna when he was 25. There he began teaching, publishing his compositions, and performing concerts. The young man spent his money freely and was usually in debt. In 1782 he married Con-stanze Weber against his father's wishes, and father and son began a battle that would haunt the composer for the rest of his life. Leopold Mozart realized that his son could not handle money and had a hard time dealing with other people; his letters to his child were full of fatherly advice. Mozart usually did not take this advice.

All of Mozart's powerful works are perfect examples of the **Classical era** of music. After an illness that was never diagnosed, Mozart suddenly died at age 35. He was buried in a pauper's grave, and its location is unknown. His extraordinary music influenced many later composers.

 A performance of Mozart's Requiem Mass in D Minor. Mozart (seated with blanket) became ill while composing the piece, which was the last one he wrote. Library of Congress LC-USZ62-69168

opportunities that came his way. His Mutti would be so proud of his accomplishments, and he could write her long letters with all the details about his experiences in Vienna, especially the hours he would spend with Mozart. Even his father would be excited by such an achievement. No doubt Johann would brag to his friends and neighbors about his oldest son becoming Mozart's pupil.

It was springtime in Vienna, and Beethoven was hoping for a meeting with Mozart. Neefe was sure that Mozart would ask the 16-year-old to become a student after hearing him perform.

🎵 Wolfgang Amadeus Mozart. Library of Congress

The Viennese Waltz

The Viennese waltz was a very popular ball-room dance in 18th-century Austria. This dance developed out of an Italian folk dance that was called the *volta*, meaning "turn." In German-speaking countries the dance became known as a waltz, which in German means to glide and to turn. By the 17th century this peasant dance evolved into a graceful swirl of aristocrats around the ballroom floor.

Some people considered the waltz sinful and immoral. Viennese waltzes required closer body contact than the other dances that were fashionable during this era, such as the **minuet** or the polonaise, which kept the dancers at arm's length. The waltz required that the man place his arm around his partner, causing them to stand quite close to each other. In addition, the rapid turns required that women clasp and lift their gowns to avoid tripping on them or having the gown stepped on by their partner. This meant that the women had to display their ankles, which was considered indecent by some. In spite of this disapproval, the waltz's popularity grew, and by the middle of the 1700s aristocrats enjoyed the dance so much that it became a major feature during their formal balls.

In the 1800s there were several composers who specialized in writing waltz music. Joseph Lanner and Johann Strauss II are best known for their beautiful waltzes. Today there are several recognized versions of the dance including the American and International styles. Many waltz competitions and ballroom dancers keep the tradition of the waltz alive.

Dance a Viennese Waltz

THE VIENNESE waltz was first danced in the 18th century and was based on an Austrian folk dance. The word "waltz" comes from the German word for "turn," and the dance features many turns while gliding across the floor.

You'll Need

∞ Dance partner

∞ CD or MP3 download of a Viennese waltz such as *The Blue Danube* by Johann Strauss

∞ Music-listening device (such as an iPod, computer, or CD player)

Note: There are many versions of the Viennese waltz on YouTube.

The waltz is danced in ¾ time: a one-two-three beat. The most common dance step in the waltz is called the "box step" because you move in the shape of a square.

1. One person leads; facing each other, join hands with your partner.

2. The person leading the dance places his or her right hand on the partner's waist. The partner places his or her left hand on the leader's right shoulder.

3. The partner's steps are the mirror image of the leader's steps. Both dancers' heads should be turned in the same direction as their feet turn.

4. Both partners stand straight and count to the beats of the music.

5. The box step is divided into two parts—a forward half box and a backward half box. Each half box has three steps—a step forward or backward, a step to the side, and a step to close the feet together.

6. The leader begins with the left foot and executes a forward half box followed by a backward half box. The partner performs the opposite, starting with the right foot, a backward half box followed by a forward half box.

7. Both partners repeat the steps to form a box.

8. The basic box step pattern uses three counts—one, two, three; slow, quick, quick—which is repeated twice to create the box step.

9. Once both dancers have mastered the box step, they can add turns and their own flourishes, keeping the dance soft and smooth.

🎔 Nine positions of the waltz.

Correct Method of German and French Waltzing by Thomas Wilson, 1816

Make Austrian Apple Pancakes

AUSTRIAN PANCAKES are baked in the oven, not cooked on a griddle or in a frying pan.

Adult supervision required

You'll Need

∞ 2 9-inch round baking pans
∞ ¼ cup butter, melted
∞ 4 eggs
∞ ½ teaspoon salt
∞ ¾ cup all-purpose flour
∞ ¾ cup milk
∞ 2 medium cored apples, thinly sliced
∞ ¼ cup granulated sugar
∞ ¼ teaspoon ground cinnamon

1. Preheat the oven to 400 degrees.

2. Coat the bottom and sides of the pans with a bit of the melted butter to grease them.

3. To make the batter, combine the eggs, salt, flour, milk, and melted butter in a bowl, and mix well until smooth.

4. Arrange half of the apple slices in each pan. Cover the apples with the batter, dividing the batter equally between each pan.

5. Mix the sugar with the cinnamon and sprinkle two tablespoons over the batter in each pan.

6. Bake for 20 to 25 minutes until the Austrian apple pancakes are golden brown.

Serves four.

But Ludwig understood that things could happen that would change this exciting plan. What if Mozart did not like his music? What if he made mistakes during his performance? What if he said the wrong things and angered important people? His father had warned him, "God gave you two ears and only one mouth. Listen twice as much as you talk." The young man waited in the beautiful city known for its art and culture, magnificent palaces, delicious pastries, and grand balls.

There is no trustworthy account about what happened when Beethoven performed for Mozart. But we do know the young musician's inventiveness and ability to improvise impressed Mozart greatly, causing Mozart to comment, "Keep an eye on him—someday he will give the world something to talk about."

Letter from Bonn

AN INVITATION to meet with Beethoven again or to become one of Mozart's pupils did not arrive. Beethoven valiantly tried to control his impatience and to think about other things. The beautiful city that surrounded him certainly offered plenty of distractions. The young man enjoyed good food and loved to take long walks, and Vienna offered both. After a hearty breakfast of delicious Viennese goodies like apple pancakes and buttermilk, one could hike the wide boulevards, cobblestone side streets, and narrow alleyways, passing grand palaces with splendid gardens, churches with tall spires, and pleasant parks.

But even the sights and sounds of Vienna would not, at this trying time, have cheered Beethoven. His worst fears had become reality: it appeared that Mozart was not interested in him, and perhaps he would never be. Was it all a hopeless daydream? Should he give up or think of another plan? What should or could he do to attract Mozart's attention so that he could become one of his pupils? Full of so many doubts and questions, Beethoven returned to his lodgings. And then an unexpected letter arrived. It was from his father, telling him that his mother was gravely ill and not expected to live much longer. Mutti had tuberculosis. "Come back to Bonn as quickly as you can," the letter urged. Beethoven had to find the money for the coach fare and get back home.

Disappointed by what had happened in Vienna and frightened about what was happening at home, Beethoven felt like his mind was in a blur during the return voyage to Bonn. Each kilometer seemed to take forever. Would he arrive home in time to see his dying mother? He entered the house that was already shrouded in sadness. His mother was lying in her thick featherbed looking very thin and weak. Beethoven held her delicate hand in his larger one. He prayed for his mother's recovery, but it was not to be. She passed away on July 17, 1787. Her death was a terrible blow to the family. A few years later Beethoven wrote to a friend in Bonn, "Who was happier than I when I could still pronounce the sweet word 'mother' and have it heard? To whom can I speak it now?"

As soon as they returned from the cemetery after Mutti's burial, Johann left the house and headed for the nearest tavern. The strain of his wife's illness and death caused him to drink even more. Soon after the loss of his wife, Johann lost his job. His oldest son had to take over the role of the only breadwinner and provide for his brothers, Caspar Carl and Nikolaus Johann. Beethoven went to his teacher to explain the situation. Neefe offered to have him continue his job as organist and also play the viola in the theater orchestra. Beethoven's Bonn students resumed their music lessons, but what he earned was not enough to support a family. Though just 17, he petitioned the elector to be recognized as the head of the household and to pay him one half of his father's former salary so that they all could survive. This petition was granted.

The French Revolution Begins

Two years after Mutti's death, the family finances were finally under control and 19-year-old Beethoven started to think about his limited

The French Revolution

A person's status in European society was determined by birth. The highest class, whose members lived in luxury, was the nobility, which ruled the people. The second-highest position was held by the clergy. The majority of the people, the commoners, were the lowest social class and did not have any power. In France these classes were called the "three estates."

In the late 1700s France faced an economic crisis, and people were starving. Some French citizens believed that their society could be improved while retaining a portion of the established system. Looking toward reform, King Louis XVI, the nobility, and the clergy agreed to establish the Estates General, consisting of members of the nobility, the church, and representatives of the common people. The Estates General met in May 1789. The delegates for the third estate, the common people, complained that they should have more votes since they represented the largest group of people. Disheartened, they soon broke away from the Estates General and formed the National Assembly.

Social tensions rose as news of the attempt at reform trickled down to the lowest class. When the peasants learned that the hated Bastille prison had been attacked, they were certain that the time had come for social change. In the summer of 1789 hundreds of thousands of peasants burned the fields and assaulted the manor houses of the noblity, which stood as symbols of oppression. They demanded a constitution that would guarantee rights for all. By the end of the summer, the Declaration of the Rights of Man was adopted by the National Assembly. It established fundamental rights for French citizens but did not include women's rights or an end to slavery. Four years later, in 1793, Louis XVI was executed, and the absolute monarchy that had ruled France was gone. French society was reorganized. Feudal customs were eliminated, and often talent replaced birth as a determining factor in a person's social status.

education. Beethoven had enjoyed the world of literature that the von Breunings' library had offered to him and began attending classes at the University of Bonn. The courses focused on the giants of German literature: Johann Wolfgang von Goethe and Johann Christoph Friedrich von Schiller. Both men were known for their philosophy and for their poetry. Schiller's epic poem entitled "Ode to Joy," which celebrated the ideal of unity and brotherhood of all humankind, remained in Beethoven's heart.

Beethoven had just heard that in Paris, France, on July 14, 1789, a huge mob of French people had stormed the Bastille prison, an ancient fortress that housed political prisoners. The attack on the thick-walled fortress was a result of the people's

❀ The Bastille before its destruction.

Music Notes: What Are Opus Numbers?

"**Opus**" is a Latin word meaning "work." The abbreviation "op." is used for "opus," and "no." is the abbreviation for "number." In the 17th century, publishers and composers started using opus numbers to identify musical works. Usually opus numbers correspond to the order in which a work was *written*, though occasionally they signify instead the order in which the work was *published*. For example, op. 1 would be the composer's first published work. Some of Beethoven's earliest works were never assigned an opus number and are listed as WoO—an abbreviation of the German term meaning "without opus number."

If several works are published at the same time, they are given an opus number and sometimes a second number to show the order in which each work was printed. For example, three Beethoven piano **concertos**—orchestral compositions in which one instrument, or solo, stands out—were assigned opus numbers by his publisher: op. 1 no. 1 is the Piano Trio in E-flat, Op. 1 no. 2 is the Piano Trio in G. And op. 1 no. 3 is the Piano Trio in C Minor. All three concertos were published at the same time, and the order in which each piece was printed is indicated by the second number. Unpublished works do not usually have an opus number. Beethoven wrote 138 pieces that were assigned opus numbers; works that did not have an opus number assigned to them are listed as WoO.

anger at being ruled by an absolute monarchy. The French Revolution had begun. The drama of the French people rising up and demanding freedom excited and moved Beethoven deeply. The stirring words of their motto crying out for "liberty, equality, and brotherhood" made a serious impression on those people still living under the iron rule of the nobility.

During his free time Beethoven walked to the Zehrgarten, a bookshop and tavern on the Marketplace in Bonn, where many educated minds gathered to discuss and debate important philosophical ideas. Beethoven thoroughly enjoyed listening to these lively discussions. A few times he ventured to add his own thoughts about freedom and the equality of all people to the conversations. Late at night, on his walk back home, he would think about all the ideas that had been considered by the debaters and the political changes happening in Europe. Beethoven thoroughly believed in a world that gave all people basic freedoms and equality before the law; he was deeply affected by the revolutionary spirit that floated in the European air.

In 1790, when Beethoven was 20, Emperor Joseph II died. He had been the ruling monarch of both the Austrian and the Holy Roman Empire. Joseph II had been regarded as an enlightened, fair-minded ruler. He had abolished the forced labor of peasants on landowners' property, called "serfdom," and established religious reforms. Beethoven was asked to compose music for a memorial ceremony to be held in the emperor's memory. He wrote a piece for orchestra, soloists, and chorus employing the words of a poem supplied by the members of the Bonn Reading Society, which was sponsoring the memorial. The **cantata** (a composition for one or more voices with instrumental **accompaniment**) displayed Beethoven's technical skills with haunting melodies and great energy. But for some reason this *Cantata on the Death of Emperor Joseph II* (WoO 87) was not performed at the ceremony. Some scholars say that this was due to the technical difficulty of the work, and others say that there was not enough time to rehearse such a lengthy piece.

The next emperor ruled for less than two years and was followed by his son, Emperor Francis II, who was not an enlightened ruler. This monarch was suspicious of everyone and distrusted anyone who might disagree with him. The French Revolution and its humanitarian ideals frightened him—he feared that any political reform would take away from his power. The ideals of the Enlightenment worried this emperor so much that they caused him to enact strict and controlling laws intended to keep his subjects from rebelling against his rule. Francis II decided that Beethoven's views on freedom and equality

🎔 Emperor Joseph II. Courtesy of Marcus Kaar, portrait.kaar.at

were too radical for him and was quoted as saying, "There is something revolutionary in that music."

As each year passed, Beethoven's personal world was expanding. The people of Bonn were hearing and enjoying his music and his performances. Through the von Breuning family he was able to meet a few powerful and wealthy people who became interested in helping him. Count Ferdinand von Waldstein and Christian Neefe were both a constant source of encouragement. As the young man entered adulthood, his life was beginning to look more promising, and Beethoven looked forward to the future.

4

ACCLAIM IN VIENNA

"If you want to know whether you have written anything worth preserving, sing it to yourself without any accompaniment."
—JOSEPH HAYDN

THE FAMOUS COMPOSER Joseph Haydn was passing through Bonn on his way to London in July 1792. Haydn was known throughout Europe, and his music was well loved. He was called "the father of the **symphony**" because his symphonic works were so magnificently constructed. A symphony is a large-scale work for orchestra in several parts called "movements." Haydn created movements that were dynamic and brilliant. Written over his lifetime, his symphonies number over 100, and each one was well planned and unified musically.

Although some people thought they were rivals, Haydn and Mozart had actually been friends, and Haydn was very shocked and upset by the untimely and unfortunate death

Joseph Haydn. *Two Hundred German Men* by Bechstein, 1854; courtesy of Marcus Kaar, portrait.kaar.at

of the younger composer the previous December. Mozart had frequently commented that he'd learned how to write string **quartets** from Haydn and had often called Haydn his teacher. The two composers had great respect for each other. After Mozart's death Haydn wrote, "Scarcely any man can brook comparison with the great Mozart.... If I could only impress on the soul of every friend of music, and on high personages in particular, how inimitable are Mozart's works, how profound, how musically intelligent, how extraordinarily sensitive!" Haydn had said to Mozart's father, "I consider your son the greatest composer I know."

When Joseph Haydn stopped off in Bonn, all of the important townspeople came to see him. Haydn's presence made one of Beethoven's patrons realize that he had the chance to promote his young protégé to the elderly musician. Armed with Beethoven's work, he went to see the famous man. After a few words of introduction and welcome, Beethoven's patron handed Haydn a copy of the *Cantata on the Death of Emperor Joseph II.* The celebrated composer looked at the **manuscript** carefully.

"Who wrote this?" he asked. "It is very good."

The patron explained that a young man from Bonn had recently composed the cantata. Haydn was so impressed by the composition that he immediately invited Beethoven to come to Vienna to study with him. The patron could hardly wait to inform Beethoven about this fantastic opportunity. He rushed over to see him and give him the fabulous news.

Leaving Bonn

BEETHOVEN WAS surprised by Haydn's invitation and felt both happy and anxious about such a wonderful possibility. He thought about it for quite a while before agreeing to leave his family and go to Vienna. Beethoven had spent five years supporting his brothers, but now they were almost grown and were pursuing their own careers. Caspar Carl had become a musician, and Nikolaus Johann was in the middle of his apprenticeship to become a pharmacist. As for his father, Beethoven realized that he could not do anything to change or improve Johann's life. Here was the chance to go to a large and culturally vibrant city that could offer 22-year-old Beethoven so much more than his hometown.

He decided to go. The problem was how to pay for the move to Vienna and for his studies. Beethoven did not have a way to accomplish this on his own. Luckily, after learning about Haydn's offer, Count Ferdinand von Waldstein, the elector and Beethoven's patron who had accompanied him on his first trip to Vienna five years earlier, volunteered to pay for Beethoven's return to Vienna.

❀ Joseph Haydn. *Two Hundred German Men* by Bechstein, 1854; courtesy of Marcus Kaar, portrait.kaar.at

On a brisk November day many of Beethoven's friends and admirers came to say good-bye to him and wish him well. In his cloth satchel Beethoven carried a letter of introduction from the count that ended with the words: "Through your unfailing efforts, receive Mozart's spirit from Haydn's hands. Your true friend, Waldstein." This valuable letter of introduction would

Joseph Haydn

Joseph Haydn, the second child of a wagon wheel maker and a former court cook, was born in a village in Austria in 1732. When his parents became aware that their child had remarkable musical gifts, they contacted a relative who was a schoolmaster and choirmaster in the town of Hainburg. This relative took in the six-year-old and placed him in school, where Haydn studied the violin and the harpsichord. He also sang in the church choir, where he was noticed by a **Kapellmeister**, or choir director, in Vienna, who brought Haydn to the city to sing in his church choir.

In 1760, Haydn was employed by the Hungarian prince Esterházy. Soon Haydn was the Kapellmeister for the court orchestra; he remained in that position for almost 30 years. During that time Haydn composed music for the festivities, church services, and concerts that were held at the palace.

He wrote 60 symphonies, 30 sonatas, 11 **operas**, and many other works during his employment with the Esterházy family.

Haydn returned to Vienna in 1795. There he began to compose **oratorios**, which are large choral works. His oratorios *The Creation* and *The Seasons* are considered to be his final masterpieces. Haydn's sense of humor can be glimpsed in Symphony no. 94, the *Surprise* Symphony, where there is an unexpected, loud chord that shocks the audience in the second movement, and in his Symphony no. 101, nicknamed the *Clock* because the second movement has a ticking rhythm.

In 1808, Haydn collapsed after a performance of *The Creation*. As he was being carried out of the concert hall, Beethoven came to his side and kissed his hands. Haydn passed away a year later. At a memorial service for the composer, Mozart's *Requiem* was performed.

Write a Letter of Introduction

BEETHOVEN'S LETTER of introduction from Count von Waldstein paved the way for his move to Vienna. A letter of introduction is a formal letter that presents you or someone else to another person. It is a way of getting "a foot in the door." It may be used to try to get a job or make social contacts. Try writing a letter of introduction for yourself, a friend, or a sibling that you hand to a possible employer (perhaps a neighbor or friend of your parents) for a job, such as babysitting or doing yard work.

You'll Need

∞ Scratch paper
∞ Pen
∞ Stationery
∞ Computer and printer (optional)

On the scratch paper, write down some important facts about yourself or the person you are introducing:

∞ If you are writing about someone other than yourself, how do you know this person?
∞ The subject's strengths
∞ Age, grade in school
∞ Interests, hobbies, best school subjects
∞ Previous experience, such as taking care of younger relatives, doing yard work at home, working in a school garden, or any other jobs or home chores
∞ Any relevant courses that the subject of the letter has taken, such as a first-aid course, a babysitting class, or a gardening or nature class
∞ Complimentary comments about the person

Begin with the date, your address, and a greeting. Next, use your notes to write the letter, providing facts and complimentary comments about the person. Keep the letter brief—two or three paragraphs. End with "Sincerely, [Your signature]"

If you use a computer, remember to sign your name in ink.

Today's Date

Your Street Address
Your City, State, Zip Code

To Whom It May Concern:

The purpose of this letter is to introduce Marlene Jones, who is looking for a job as an assistant camp counselor. Marlene is now twelve years old and in the seventh grade. She has made the honor roll every year and is vice president of her class in middle school.

Marlene has been our neighbor for about nine years. She often invites me and my sister over to her house to play. We like to go to her home because she has several pets, including a ferret and a big dog. She also has lots of interesting games and craft projects.

Marlene is very creative and enjoys making things. She can play the piano, paint, and knit. One day last year she tried to teach me how to knit, but I kept dropping the stitches. She was very patient and a good teacher. I think she would be a good assistant counselor for your camp.

Sincerely,

Adrianne Smith

allow Beethoven to connect with important people.

The count had also set up a fund that would help Beethoven pay for the stagecoach journey to Vienna and his expenses when he arrived. Travel was dangerous; the new French regime had declared war on Austria, and their armies were marching toward each other. French forces had already reached the Rhine when Beethoven stepped into the coach. All the passengers were nervous about the war that was frighteningly close by. They were lucky to reach Vienna without any incident.

A few weeks after arriving in Vienna, Beethoven received a letter from his brothers telling him that their father had passed away. The news saddened him, but he was comforted by the fact that he had done all he could for his family. Although his brothers were on their way to being able to support themselves, if all worked out in Vienna, he would send them some money from time to time to help them out.

Haydn and Beethoven Clash

And so Beethoven became one of Haydn's students. The great difference in their ages and their conflicting personalities quickly affected their relationship. Haydn noticed that his young pupil continually looked sloppy and shabby and did not seem to care about his appearance. His clothing was usually informal, soiled, and wrinkled and his hair was often in need of a trim or at least a thorough brushing. This seeming carelessness on the part of his student bothered Haydn, who proudly sported stylish clothes, spotless silk stockings, and elegant shoes, all topped by a carefully powdered wig. But the teacher recognized that his difficult pupil was brilliant, kindhearted, and extremely talented. Once, when Beethoven asked Haydn to comment on his work and himself, Haydn observed, "You make upon me the impression of a man who has several heads, several hearts, and several souls."

The teacher also disapproved of Beethoven's independent attitude and hot temper. Haydn felt that Beethoven was often impatient and unreasonable and did not seem to care or understand that Haydn had other students to teach, music to be composed and orchestrated, and concerts to attend. Most of his pupils called him Papa Haydn and seemed to feel honored to be studying with him. He frequently thought that Beethoven's voice was too harsh and his laugh was too loud. This young man was far too restless to follow his proven, clear-cut musical formulas and sage advice. Often the older man would picture himself pulling on Beethoven's unruly hair and telling him to go find another composer with whom to take his lessons. Haydn believed that Beethoven made no effort to please him or, for that matter, anyone else.

Johann Georg Albrechtsberger. Reproduced with permission of the Ira F. Brilliant Center for Beethoven Studies, San José State University

Beethoven quickly realized that Haydn could not give him the attention that he thought he deserved. He made the comment that he had "not found that excellence which he supposed he had a right to expect" from this teacher. Student and instructor often clashed. Their raised voices echoed and bounced through the corners and corridors of the building. Beethoven was very displeased that Haydn had little time to spend with him. But even more, he disliked his demanding and confining method of instruction. Haydn insisted on the importance of endless lessons in the rules of **counterpoint** (combining melodies) and constant exercises in writing counterpoint. Beethoven believed that counterpoint was an overrated method of musical development left over from the **Baroque era** of the past. Haydn also insisted that the young composer study previous composers' works rather than composing new pieces. Beethoven saw little value in repeating these same, fruitless drills and methods day after day.

About one year after accepting Beethoven as his student, Haydn announced that he was leaving Vienna for London. To make up for this move, Haydn contacted other famous Viennese musicians about his pupil. They responded that they would be glad to work with a gifted young man. Beethoven wanted his parting with Haydn to be on good terms. In his notebook he wrote that before Haydn left, he took his teacher out to a cafe for chocolate and a cup of coffee.

With Haydn away in England, Beethoven began his studies with the music theorist and composer Johann Georg Albrechtsberger three times a week. Albrechtsberger mentioned that his new student was stubborn and tended to learn more through experience than through his instruction. In this era the composition of music followed definite and strict rules; Beethoven preferred to ignore these traditional conventions or, at least, to bend them to suit his own ideas. Beethoven had learned the accepted musical formulas that his teachers followed, but he rejected the idea that these were rigid rules that could not be altered. Albrechtsberger stressed attention to detail, and this made his pupil constantly strive to improve what he composed.

Beethoven and the Aristocrats

BEETHOVEN ENJOYED the attention of the members of the ruling class and often participated in the concerts, called "salons," which were held in their handsome mansions. The composer expected the members of the nobility to treat him as an equal. He explained his thinking: "It is good to move among the aristocracy but it is first necessary to make them respect you." His desire to be treated as an equal by the nobility caused Beethoven to mislead some people. In German, "von" in a name indicated that a person was a member of the nobility. Beethoven did not correct people who thought the "van" in his name meant that he was born into an upper-class family, even though his name really followed the Flemish style and simply meant "from." Beethoven enjoyed the idea that some highborn people believed that royal blood also flowed in his veins.

The aristocrats enjoyed his powerful performances and often became his patrons and students. Beethoven dedicated many of his works to these patrons who supported him throughout his life. But he also upset and displeased a number of them with his blunt, rough way of talking and his quick anger. When one of the noblemen attending a salon concert kept talking during one of Beethoven's recitals, the performer stopped playing, stood up, and loudly stated, "For such pigs, I do not play!" before angrily striding out of the room.

One of Vienna's most important patrons of the arts was Prince Karl Lichnowsky, who gave the composer a room in his home soon after Beethoven first arrived in the city. Lichnowsky and his wife invited the young man to perform at their Friday evening salons, giving Beethoven the opportunity to meet wealthy, influential people. Beethoven was quite annoyed that living in the same house as the royal couple required that he pay attention to the cleanliness of his clothes, dress properly, arrive punctually for meals, and

Beethoven's Patrons

In Bonn, Beethoven's first patron was the Austrian nobleman Count Ferdinand Ernst Gabriel von Waldstein, who was fascinated by the arts. The count financed Beethoven's return to Vienna and made certain that he would meet the right people to further his career there. Another early patron was the elector of Cologne, Maximilian Franz, whose sister was Queen Marie Antoinette of France. Beethoven played in Maximilian Franz's orchestra, and the elector was the one who invited Joseph Haydn to Bonn.

Archduke Rudolph was the youngest son of Emperor Leopold II. Beethoven was his piano and composition teacher. The archduke showcased some of Beethoven's works at his court and kept up a lively correspondence with the composer. The men were good friends for many years.

In 1805, Beethoven wrote a letter calling Prince Karl Lichnowsky "one of my most faithful friends and one of the most loyal patrons of my music." After Beethoven's arrival in Vienna, the music-loving prince allowed the young man to live in his palace and paid him a generous yearly salary for six years. Their relationship soured when Beethoven refused to perform for visiting French officers in Prince Lichnowsky's palace.

Prince Franz Joseph Maximilian von Lobkowitz's palace salon was large enough for full orchestral performances, and he maintained his own orchestra. The prince was a friend of Count von Waldstein. For years he was another patron contributing to the annual salary that Beethoven collected, until the war with France bankrupted the prince and he left Vienna.

Beethoven often dedicated his music to these patrons, but his independent attitude caused problems. Many patrons were willing to overlook Beethoven's difficult personality, knowing that his music was brilliant. Beethoven needed these patrons to advance his career and support him until he could earn enough money on his own.

behave like a gracious guest. This situation often distressed him and put him in a terrible mood. Resentful of the expectations and social graces of the aristocrats, Beethoven said to his friend Wegeler, "Am I supposed to come home every day at half-past three, change my clothes, shave, and all that? I'll have none of it!"

Soon he decided that he had to move out of his patron's house and into a home of his own, but all he could afford was a small room. He would also have to buy some furniture, dishes, linens, and his own piano. Earning enough money to be able to achieve this goal would be a problem and a constant worry even with the allowances from his patrons. Yet, it would give him the freedom to be himself.

Beethoven entered many piano competitions. These competitions focused on the glory of winning and did not have a monetary prize. Beethoven always won because he had great improvisational skills, which meant that he could take a basic melody and build other melodies out of it. The ability to improvise was widely admired during this era. One famous competition was against Abbot Joseph Gelinek, who had challenged the young man to a musical duel. After the competition the abbot commented to one of Beethoven's pupils, Carl Czerny, that Beethoven "displayed difficulties and effects on the piano beyond anything of which we might have dreamed."

As the 18th century neared its end, the social order in Europe was rapidly changing. Now that the merchant and professional classes could afford some luxuries, they were buying instruments, musical scores to play on these instruments, and tickets to public concerts, which were becoming very popular as entertainment. Musicians and artists did not need to rely on their wealthy patrons as their only source of income anymore. Beethoven's music was in high demand; in fact, he was well on his way to becoming a celebrity. Around this time Beethoven

✽ Abbot Joseph Gelinek. Reproduced with permission of the Ira F. Brilliant Center for Beethoven Studies, San José State University

Create a CD Cover for a Beethoven Work

CD COVERS provide information about the music. An attractive cover makes people want to buy the CD and listen to the work. Try your hand at designing a Beethoven CD cover. For inspiration, listen to the Beethoven composition you have chosen while working on your CD cover.

You'll Need

∞ A Beethoven composition on CD

∞ Music-listening device (such as an iPod, computer, or CD player)

∞ Pencil

∞ Several sheets of scratch paper

∞ Scissors

∞ 1 sheet stiff sketchbook paper

∞ Ruler

∞ Colored markers or poster paints

1. Listen to the composition you have chosen a few times. What enters your thoughts while listening to the music? What image do you think would make other people want to listen to this music? A piano or other instrument? Music notes? A picture of Beethoven? Or perhaps something more abstract?

2. On the scratch paper, make pencil sketches of your image until you are happy with it.

3. Try out some interesting lettering for the written information.

4. Think about which colors would best express the music.

5. Plan where you will place the final image, the title of the work, and the names of the composer, orchestra, and conductor.

6. When you are happy with your design plan, cut your sketchbook paper into a 5-by-4½-inch rectangle; this is your CD cover.

7. Now transfer your design onto the CD cover.

8. Use the ruler and pencil to draw lines for the writing, and add your text. Re-create your image in pencil.

9. Use the markers or paints to add color.

10. Slip your new cover over the current CD cover inside the case. Now the music is truly your own!

wrote to his friend Wegeler, "My compositions are bringing in a goodly sum, and, I may add, it is scarcely possible for me to execute the orders given." Publishers were vying for the opportunity to print and sell Beethoven's works, he was performing at concerts, and he had several patrons—his financial condition was definitely improving.

In 1795 three Beethoven piano concertos were assigned opus numbers by the 25-year-old's publisher. Opus 1 no. 1 is the Piano Trio in E-flat; Opus 1 no. 2 is the Piano Trio in G, and Opus 1 no. 3 is the Piano Trio in C Minor. All three of these concertos were dedicated to Prince Lichnowsky, who had recently granted the composer an annual allowance of 600 florins, a very generous amount of money.

Prince Lichnowsky was one of Beethoven's greatest and most helpful patrons. He was an accomplished amateur musician and enjoyed participating in **chamber concerts**. Prince Lichnowsky was busy arranging a concert tour and would accompany the composer to Berlin, Prague, Dresden, and Leipzig. The prince had arranged a similar concert tour for Mozart some years before. In these major European cities Beethoven would perform for the aristocracy and also for the public.

Beethoven was pleased to learn that he would have the time to continue to write music while on this tour. He dedicated two cello sonatas to King Friedrich Wilhelm II of Prussia, who rewarded the composer with a small box filled with gold coins. The tour was very successful, and Beethoven was called a **virtuoso**, meaning "someone with great ability." Beethoven noted that these concerts provided him with "a good deal of money," and upon his return to Vienna he was able to move to his own apartment.

Musical Architect

BEETHOVEN USED notebooks to plan out his music much like an architect plans a building. In them he worked out his ideas and carefully molded each piece until it reached its final form. The notebooks demonstrate how the composer experimented with his ideas. He would begin with a set of notes that became the groundwork of the piece and then begin to build harmonies around these notes. Almost every **measure** (a fixed number of beats contained within two vertical lines on a **staff**) was written and rewritten even though he heard the complete music in his head, developing it for long periods of time before putting it on paper. He would continue altering the music and the **orchestration** until it seemed perfect to him.

Beethoven explained his creative thinking process to another musician, Louis Schlösser, in this way:

I carry my thoughts about me for a long time, often a very long time, before I write them down; meanwhile my memory is so faithful that I am sure never to forget, not even in years, a theme that has once occurred to me. I change many things, discard, and try again until I am satisfied. Then, however, there begins in my head the development in every direction, and, in as much as I know exactly what I want, the fundamental idea never deserts me, it arises before me, grows, I see and hear the picture in all its extent and dimensions stand before my mind like a cast, and there remains for me nothing but the labor of writing it down, which is quickly accomplished when I have the time, for I sometimes take up other work, but never to the confusion of one with the other.

You will ask me where I get my ideas. That I cannot tell you with certainty; they come unsummoned, directly, indirectly, I could seize them with my hands, out in the open air; in the woods; while walking; in the silence of the nights; early in the morning; incited by moods, which are translated by the poet into words, by me into tones that sound, and roar and storm about me until I have set them down in notes.

Unfortunately, because of his method of writing and rewriting, Beethoven's work was quite sloppy and hard to read. His brother Caspar Carl, who had recently moved to Vienna, care-fully copied the manuscripts for the publishers since Ludwig's **notation** was so difficult to read. Getting assistance from his musician brother was a wonderful benefit for Beethoven, who was pleased to have him nearby. However, these good feelings changed when Beethoven learned that Caspar Carl had tried to sell some of his own compositions to Beethoven's publishers by telling them that they were his older brother's work. This

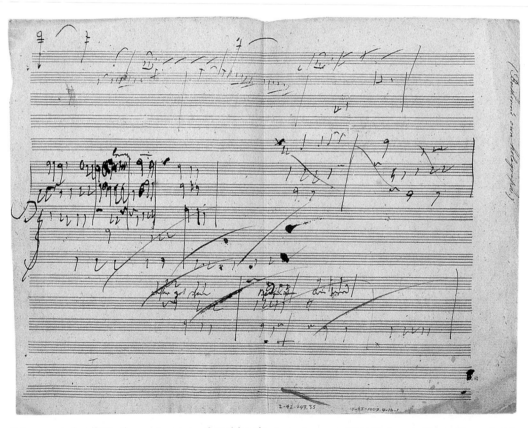

✿ **An example of Beethoven's messy sketchbook.** Library of Congress, The Moldenhauer Archives molden.2428111 bib

deception caused several big arguments between them and strained their relationship almost to breaking them apart.

Publishers began competing for the rights to publish his works. By the time Beethoven was 31 he was in a position to write, "I have six or seven publishers for each of my works and could have more if I chose. No more bargaining. I name my terms and they pay." This created a unique situation for Beethoven, who was the first composer able to earn an income by selling his compositions and by providing concerts for the public.

Beethoven was extremely pleased that the public was eager to attend his concerts and that his published music was so popular. Although many patrons were still willing to sponsor him, he often sighed with relief that he could earn money in other ways and did not have to be dependent on his patrons' goodwill, live in their courts, follow their rules, or compose the specific pieces of music that they requested from him.

On April 2, 1800, Beethoven's Symphony no. 1 in C Major (op. 21) **premiered** in the majestic Burgtheater on Michaelerplatz in Vienna. Three of Mozart's operas had premiered there, and the emperor Joseph II had proclaimed this building as the German National Theater. Beethoven had often admired the architecture of this stately structure during his frequent long walks in this area. He was looking forward to this particular **debut**.

The composer had worked on this symphony for five years. Haydn had stressed learning symphonic form, and Beethoven had learned a great deal about writing this type of work from his former teacher. As he walked to the middle of the stage, Beethoven glanced at the audience seated

Music Notes: What Is a Symphony?

The word "symphony" comes from the Greek word *sumphónia*, which means "harmonious." A symphony is a grand, extended musical work for an orchestra. Early symphonies were written in three movements, but by the Classical era they usually contained four movements and could have as many as five. A movement is a self-contained piece of music that is separated from the other movements in the symphony by silence. The movements of a symphony contrast with one another in **tempo**, mood, and character.

By 1760 classical symphonies followed a certain pattern: the first movement employed a fast tempo, usually in sonata form, while the second movement was written in a slower tempo. An elegant dance, like the minuet, was often employed in the third movement. Normally the **finale** or final movement was written in a faster tempo. Later composers created their own variations of this basic formula. Symphonies were popular vehicles for presenting an instrumental major work and are performed by large instrumental **ensembles** called "symphony orchestras."

Beethoven's first two symphonies followed the traditions that had been established by earlier composers; soon after, he changed and expanded the symphony. His third, the *Eroica*, is double the length of any symphonies that were written before. His *Choral* Symphony was the first to use voices in this form. Beethoven enjoyed writing this type of work. He said, "Symphonies are the best representation of my true self. I always seem to hear within me the sounds of a great orchestra."

in the magnificent hall waiting for him to begin conducting the premiere of his first symphony. Hundreds of eyes returned his gaze.

It was the very beginning of a new century, and echoes of Haydn and Mozart bounced throughout the notes of the first two movements. The conductor was aware that in the next movement he was about to stamp his own alteration on the previously sacred symphonic traditions of the older masters. Until the third movement began, the audience was completely comfortable with the music they had come to hear. And then, suddenly, they realized that Beethoven had inserted a **scherzo**—a lively composition—instead of the expected and more sedate minuet into this part of the work. The listeners were surprised; many people liked the change to tradition, but some in the audience were outraged that a composer had dared to take such liberties with the long-established traditions of a symphony. After the concert an angry critic exclaimed, "A scherzo has no place in a symphony! What right does this composer have to change the accepted and time-honored form of a symphony?"

Beethoven did not really give much thought to what the critics had to say. It seemed that the

The Burgtheater on Michaelerplatz. Library of Congress LC-DIG-ppmsc-09208

public liked his music and his publishers were clamoring for him to provide them with more. He was feeling welcome in Vienna and satisfied with his life. Then fate struck a blow to the young composer.

5

The Heiligenstadt Testament

"For the last three years my hearing has become weaker and weaker."

—Ludwig van Beethoven, in a letter to his friend Franz Wegeler, dated June 29, 1801

BEETHOVEN'S PHYSICAL APPEARANCE was as striking as his brash personality. He was no more than five feet five inches tall, with broad shoulders and large, powerful hands ending in short, muscular fingers. Although often clumsy with objects, on a keyboard these hands were capable of magnificent music. Beethoven's head was unusually large. He had a broad forehead, bushy eyebrows, square nose, cleft chin, and deep-set dark eyes. The small scars on his cheeks were evidence that he had lived through a bout with the often-deadly disease called smallpox. Thick, dark, unruly hair framed his face.

Beethoven in the Country by Julius Schmid
Reproduced with the permission of the Ira F. Brilliant Center for Beethoven Studies, San José State University

Beethoven was a dynamic man, always attempting to reach higher within himself to create music. In his diary he wrote about keeping his mind focused on his work:

Blessed is he who has overcome all passions and then proceeds energetically to perform his duties under all circumstances careless of success! Let the motive lie in the deed, not in the outcome. Be not one of those whose spring of action is the hope of reward. Do not let your life pass in inactivity. Be industrious, do your duty, banish all thoughts as to the results, be they good or evil; for such equanimity is attention to intellectual things. Seek an asylum only in Wisdom; for he who is wretched and unhappy is so only in consequence of things. The truly wise man does not concern himself with the good and evil of this world. Therefore endeavor diligently to preserve this use of your reason—for in the affairs of this world, such a use is a precious art.

Hearing Trouble

DESPITE HIS vigor and dynamism, Beethoven's health was failing him. He had noticed his hearing was growing worse over the past few years. Upon entering his 31st year, he had begun to suffer from a ringing sound in his ears. Any loud noise would cause him pain. At first, the ringing noises would start and stop, but as time passed, this annoying sound came more often and lasted longer. Beethoven was experiencing tinnitus, a condition that causes someone to constantly hear a buzzing, whistling, or ringing sound in the ears. These noises can affect one's ability to concentrate or hear actual sounds.

Thinking that he might be losing his hearing, Beethoven went to several doctors and tried all the remedies available at the time, such as ingesting strengthening medications and inserting cotton pieces doused in almond oil into his ears. But his doctors really had no treatment or cure for his condition. In the early 1800s, medical knowledge and practice were very crude. Nothing Beethoven's doctors suggested helped him.

Beethoven wrote a long letter to his boyhood friend Franz Wegeler, who was now a doctor in Bonn and married to Eleonore von Breuning, the daughter of Frau von Breuning. In Bonn, Eleonore had been Beethoven's piano pupil. The letter informed Wegeler that "for the last three years my hearing has become weaker and weaker ... the humming in my ears continues day and night without ceasing. ... To give you an idea of this extraordinary deafness, I tell you that when at the theater, I am obliged to lean forward close to the orchestra, in order to understand what is being said on the stage." He described the symptoms he was experiencing and his problem hearing high

🎵 **Beethoven in 1801.** Reproduced with the permission of the Ira F. Brilliant Center for Beethoven Studies, San José State University

notes or soft voices. Noting the fact that deafness is a serious handicap for someone in his profession, Beethoven asked that Wegeler keep this information secret.

In the letter he also described having stomach problems that his doctors could not seem to cure. This correspondence exhibits the distress and despair that Beethoven felt: "I must confess that I am living a miserable life. For almost two years I have ceased to attend any social functions, just because I find it impossible to say to people: I am deaf. If I had any other profession it would be easier, but in my profession it is a terrible handicap. As for my enemies, of whom I have a fair number, what would they say?"

The Moonlight Sonata

IN THIS letter to his friend Beethoven also mentioned that he had met a "dear charming girl who loves me and whom I love." He was writing about one of his piano students, 17-year-old Giulietta Guicciardi, who had dark blue eyes and wavy brown hair. The young lady presented her would-be suitor with a medallion portrait of herself, which was found in a secret drawer of Beethoven's desk along with three letters filled with love addressed to "My angel, my all, my very self." But Beethoven certainly knew that the countess was a part of the nobility and that he

Make a Model Eardrum

BEETHOVEN SUFFERED from tinnitus, a condition often experienced as a ringing, humming, or buzzing sound in the ears. Tinnitus usually is associated with hearing loss. Causes of this condition include ear infections, exposure to extreme noise, disease of the middle ear, or a pierced eardrum. The eardrum is a thin membrane, also called the "tympanic membrane," dividing the outer ear from the middle ear. Sound waves cause the eardrum to vibrate and send the sounds to three tiny bones in the middle ear. See how this works using an easy-to-make eardrum model.

You'll Need

- Large bowl
- Plastic wrap
- Rubber band
- Uncooked rice (about 25 grains) or fine sand
- Metal cookie sheet
- Wooden spoon
- Rattle

1. Stretch one sheet of plastic wrap over the bowl and secure it tightly in place with the rubber band. This is a model eardrum.

2. Place the rice or sand on top of the plastic wrap.

3. Hold the metal cookie sheet close to but not on the model eardrum.

4. Bang on the cookie sheet with the wooden spoon.

- What happens to the rice or sand when you make noise near it?
- What is causing the plastic wrap to vibrate?
- What happens if you make noise with a rattle near the model eardrum?
- What happens when you move the rattle farther away from the model eardrum and make noise again?

was born into a lower status. In his letter to Franz Wegeler, Beethoven commented, "Unfortunately she is not of my class."

Beethoven dedicated his Piano Sonata (op. 27, no. 2) to Countess Guicciardi. The composer added the Italian title "Quasi una fantasia," meaning "almost a fantasy," to the work. The sonata was labeled the *Moonlight* Sonata by a music critic many years later and remains one of his most famous pieces.

The work has three movements. The first movement opens with the right hand playing a series of notes while the left hand strikes an **octave** (a group of eight **tones** arranged in a pattern of steps). The second movement shifts to another **key** and contains a scherzo. This movement is

Medicine in the Early 19th Century

Medical practices in the early 19th century were based on traditional practices that had been developed without much scientific information. The Age of Enlightenment, emphasizing scientific investigation and research, was just beginning to alter the way physicians treated their patients and their ailments. Many doctors were trained through an apprenticeship and did not attend a medical school. These practitioners were taught the ancient Greek and Roman idea that diseases were caused by an imbalance of what they called the four humors of the body: blood, phlegm, black bile, and yellow bile.

Common treatments included bloodletting to rid the patient of "tainted" blood, cupping (making a small incision that drained into a heated cup placed on the skin) to remove "bad humors," and the use of a few drugs. Even aspirin was not developed until the very end of the 19th century. Drugs that we know are hazardous today, such as mercury, were commonly used. Mercury was an essential tool of the physicians in the early 19th century and was used in drugs and poultices, which were made of herbs, oils, or chemicals wrapped in cloth and applied to the skin.

In 1867, English surgeon Joseph Lister discovered the need for cleanliness in medicine. Until the 1870s it was not known that germs caused disease. Doctors did not wash their hands before touching a patient, and medical instruments were not sterilized. The chances of infection were great, and there were no antibiotics to treat it.

Although the painkilling properties of nitrous oxide were known, it was not used as an anesthetic until the middle of the century. Operations were performed while the patient was awake. Women gave birth in their homes, sometimes using midwives, and many women died in childbirth. Poor hygiene and sanitation combined with a lack of medical knowledge caused countless children to die and explained the shorter lifespan of people living in the 1800s and earlier.

fairly brief, but it serves to connect the three parts of the sonata to one another. Beethoven ends the sonata with a blazingly intense third movement featuring rapid **arpeggios** (a chord whose notes are played in rapid succession, not all together), strongly **accented** (emphasized) notes, and loud dynamics. The work was meant as a loving gift to a sweet young lady, who soon married someone else.

His ever-worsening deafness caused Beethoven to limit his public performances as well as his social life. Disappointed in love and filled with despair about losing his hearing, he decided to devote himself to composing. Beethoven became completely absorbed in his music, ignoring almost everything else, even the most basic things. Some days he did not even dress before sitting down at a **fortepiano** to compose. To compensate for his hearing loss, he had the legs of his fortepiano removed so that he could feel the vibrations of the strings with his feet as the instrument sat on the floor. The vibrations helped him to picture the music in his head.

The fortepiano was the early version of a piano used in Beethoven's time. Historians say that Beethoven never actually purchased a piano—many of the instruments he used were either borrowed or given to him. Piano manufacturers were thrilled to be able to tell their paying customers that the famous Beethoven composed or performed on an instrument that they had

The opening measures of the Piano Sonata (op. 27, no. 2), *Moonlight* Sonata. Courtesy of Susan Silberman

constructed. The manufacturers were delighted to loan or provide him with a gift of one of their latest model pianos. Beethoven's intense style of playing was so hard on the instrument that the fortepianos of the period could barely tolerate it. His instruments encountered a lot of damage due to the fact that they were not very sturdy.

Beethoven often used fortepianos made by Viennese companies, but he also liked the Broadwood models made in England. Broadwood pianos featured a more solid construction and offered more octaves. For years he worked with an Érard piano from Paris, but at one point wrote that he believed it was "quite useless." Nonetheless, Beethoven continued to use this piano until 1825. The composer was never completely

Think Like a Music Critic

CRITICS BOTH praised and criticized Beethoven's music in the newspapers and journals of his day. Music critics are journalists who write about music, performances, and performers, review concerts and new releases of CDs, and interview composers and performers. Their reviews should always be based on factual information; a music critic has to be open-minded and fair. Music critics use perceptive listening; this means listening for the elements that make up a piece of music. Listening to music like a critic helps you appreciate and understand how a composer put a work together. Try writing a review of Beethoven's famous *Moonlight* Sonata.

You'll Need

- A CD or MP3 download of the Piano Sonata (op. 27, no. 2), the *Moonlight* Sonata
- Music-listening device (such as an iPod, computer, or CD player)
- Internet or library access
- Paper and pen or word processing program

1. Go online or to the library to research what others have said about the *Moonlight* Sonata so that you can gain valuable insight about this piece.

2. Listen to the *Moonlight* Sonata several times, asking yourself the following questions. Jot down your answers and observations on the paper or type them up on the computer. Remember that the composition has three movements. You can listen to each movement separately.

- Who is performing the music?
- What are the themes, variations, repetitions, and new musical materials?
- What is the rhythm? Does it change or stay the same?
- What is the mood of the music?
- How are the various movements different or similar? Is there anything that unifies them?
- What is the composer trying to accomplish? How was this done?
- What is your reaction to the music—what did you like about it and why?
- Is there something that you did not like or would do differently?

3. Write up your critique. It can be a few paragraphs or more depending on how much you have to say. Perhaps you would like to give your review to your music teacher or submit it to your school newpaper.

satisfied with any of the instruments available to him due to their flimsy construction and short octave **range**.

A Time for Some Rest

IN THE early 1800s Heiligenstadt was a small resort town north of the city of Vienna. It was a quiet and peaceful place with lovely views of the Danube River. Beethoven's doctor suggested that he go to Heiligenstadt to get away from the pressures and stresses of his life and to get some rest. In 1802 the 32-year-old composer spent six months there. He walked through the rolling hills and dense forest, enjoying the beauties of nature and relaxing in the scenic countryside. Beethoven appreciated the calming atmosphere of these surroundings. He would sit beneath a tree for hours with his music notebook and lose all track of time. He once wrote to a friend, "No man loves the country more than I. Woods, trees and rocks give the response which man requires. Every tree seems to say 'Holy, holy.'"

Often as Beethoven strolled through the town, he was entangled in his own thoughts. People noticed that he spoke to himself during these outings. He would often stop and pull a notebook and pencil out of his pocket to scribble something down. The inhabitants of Heiligenstadt thought Beethoven's behavior was peculiar and stared at him. After a while, though, they came to believe his actions were normal for a great musician and stopped gawking at him.

In the center of town was a restaurant that offered many delicious German foods. Beethoven was especially fond of pasta with cheese on top and some of the flavorful fish dishes; he also enjoyed the sweet desserts. After one of his walks, he often returned there for a meal.

Being isolated in a small village, away from the bustling city of Vienna, gave the composer time to think about his worrisome situation. He decided that he had to inform his brothers about his thoughts and fears. Beethoven cleared papers off a table so that he could sit down to compose a letter on October 6, 1802.

The letter was in the form of a final will and is known as the "Heiligenstadt Testament." Here Beethoven revealed his deepest fears, frustration, and emotional pain during his personal crisis. He began with Caspar Carl's name but, for unknown reasons, left a space without penning in the name of his other sibling, Nikolaus Johann. Beethoven wrote this testament to his brothers with the instruction that it was to be read after his death.

He started by explaining to them that he had experienced problems with his hearing for a long time. "But, think that for six years now I have

🎜 Beethoven at his Broadwood fortepiano.

The Evolution of the Piano

In the early 1700s, Bartolomeo Cristofori, an Italian instrument maker, created a forte-piano that would have its strings struck by hammers activated by the keyboard instead of being plucked. Gottfried Silbermann, a German, invented a device that lifted the hammers off the strings, allowing them to vibrate. Sébastian Érard, a Frenchman, improved the action of the hammers, letting a note be replayed quickly.

Fortepiano eventually was replaced with the shorter name "piano." The Streicher piano company had supplied Beethoven with an instrument, but its construction was light and its sound soft. In 1818, John Broadwood and Sons, a British company, offered one of its pianos to Beethoven. Braced with iron frames, these pia-nos were sturdier and provided a larger tone. Beethoven, his hearing failing, appreciated the triple-stringed, six-octave grand piano that this company gave to him.

A modern piano has 88 keys, which provides a little more than a seven-octave span. There are three pedals, left to right: the soft pedal, una corda, allows the hammer to hit only one string instead of three; the middle pedal, called the "sostenuto pedal," sustains the notes; and the damper pedal moves the dampers off the strings to let them vibrate. Today's pianos can be built as compact uprights with the frame and the strings placed vertically or as grand pianos that are built horizontally. The piano is the most popular instrument for composing and performing.

✳ A fortepiano after Walter & Sohn, ca. 1805.
Replica by Paul McNulty

been hopelessly afflicted, made worse by sense-less physicians, from year to year deceived with hopes of improvement, finally compelled to face the prospect of a lasting malady (whose cure will take years or, perhaps, be impossible)."

He wanted to make sure that his brothers would understand. How should he make clear to them the reason why had chosen to withdraw from society and live alone? What words would describe his feelings of loneliness to Caspar Carl and Nikolaus Johann? He continued to write, "Forgive me when you see me draw back when I would gladly mingle with you. My misfortune is doubly painful because it must lead to my being misunderstood. For me there can be no recreation in the society of my fellows. I must live like an exile."

Beethoven was shamed by his disability. He could not bear to say aloud: "Speak louder, shout, for I am deaf." Believing that he could no longer engage in conversations, he had removed himself from the company of others. He ended the letter explaining that he was "brought almost to despair" by the crisis he was going through, but he also wrote that his art had saved him. "Only art it was that withheld me. Ah, it seemed impossible to leave the world until I had produced all that I felt called upon to produce, and so I endured this wretched existence."

Later, when he returned to Vienna, Beethoven hid the letter in the secret drawer of his desk. It was never sent.

Make a Thumb Piano

YOU CAN make your own musical instrument known as a "thumb piano" or a mbira. Used in African music, a mbira consists of a wooden board to which staggered metal keys have been attached. The wooden board acts like a sounding board on a piano and the metal strips act like piano keys of a piano; the **pitch** of each key is dependent on its size. The harpsichords that Beethoven used before the more modern pianos were available to him employed this plucking type of action. This instrument is fun to play.

Adult supervision required

You'll Need

- Piece of wood about 1-inch thick and cut into a 4-inch square
- Sandpaper
- Poster or acrylic paint
- Paintbrush
- 4 craft or Popsicle sticks
- White glue
- 2 rubber bands
- 4 large metal bobby pins
- Wire cutters
- Tape
- 10 pushpins

1. Sand the wood to make it smooth.

2. Paint the wood block and the craft sticks to decorate them. Since this instrument is used in Africa, you might elect to use bright, sunny colors or African symbols to decorate it. Let the paint dry thoroughly.

3. Glue two craft sticks side by side across the piece of wood, about an inch down from one of the ends.

4. Keep your thumb down in the center of the sticks and stretch the rubber bands across and underneath the wood to wrap around the ends to hold them in place while the glue dries.

5. Bend open a bobby pin to form the long key. Measure the bobby pin so that it touches the craft sticks and reaches to the end of the wood without extending over it.

6. Have an adult cut off the excess of the bobby pin with wire cutters.

7. Bend open the remaining bobby pins; cut each key a bit shorter than the one before it so that each one will have a different pitch.

8. Place the keys across the piano and tape the ends to the craft sticks to hold them in place. Apply glue across the tape.

9. Place two more craft sticks over the first two to hold the keys in place. Wrap rubber bands around the ends of these sticks to keep them in place while they dry.

10. Stick two pushpins through the craft sticks around either side of each bobby pin key all the way down through both sets of craft sticks into the wooden board to give them added strength.

11. Bend each key about ½ inch away from the wood.

12. Pluck the keys with your thumb to play the thumb piano.

Wishing for Companionship

ADDING TO the composer's depression was the fact that he never seemed to be able to find a woman with whom he could share his life. Beethoven often fell in love, but the women he chose were, for many reasons, usually unavailable for him to marry. Some of them were his pupils or wives of his patrons. Most of them were members of the aristocracy, born into a much higher social status than Beethoven. Not finding a woman to love and marry constantly disturbed the composer, whose feelings of loneliness increased each year.

Beethoven's isolation from others followed him around Heiligenstadt like a dark shadow. In his diary he wrote that he feared people would pity him or not take him seriously as a musician because of his disability. But he was determined to overcome these problems. He had written to Franz Wegeler, "With whom need I be afraid of measuring my strength? If possible I will bid defiance to my fate, although there will be moments in life when I will be the unhappiest of God's creatures. . . . I will take faith by the throat. It shall not overcome me. Oh how beautiful it is to be alive— would that I could live a thousand times!"

Beethoven in the Country by Julius Schmid Reproduced with the permission of the Ira F. Brilliant Center for Beethoven Studies, San José State University

Slowly, Beethoven came to realize that his music would have to be enough to provide him with companionship and happiness, to fulfill him and give his life purpose. He resigned himself to adjust to what he would have to face in the future.

He understood that he had to triumph over his troubles and restore his soul. Now he could return to his life in Vienna. Determined to take control of his future, Beethoven left Heiligenstadt and threw himself into his music.

The Women Beethoven Loved

Beethoven's close friend Franz Wegeler made the statement, "Beethoven was always in love with someone." To Beethoven's distress, none of these attachments was lasting.

Magdalena Willmann, an opera singer, was probably the first woman Beethoven proposed marriage to, in 1795. According to her family, Magdalena turned the composer down and one year later married a merchant.

In 1801, Beethoven dedicated his *Moonlight* Sonata to his 17-year-old student, Countess Giulietta Guicciardi. He believed that she loved him but understood that they were not social equals. In 1803, Giulietta married Count Wenzel von Gallenberg and moved to Italy. A small portrait of this young woman was later found in Beethoven's desk.

Countess Josephine Deym, a cousin of Giulietta Guicciardi, was one of Beethoven's piano students before her marriage. After she was

widowed, she returned to her former teacher to continue her lessons. Again, the fact that she was an aristocrat created a problem. If she married a commoner her four children would suffer, as the countess would have to surrender her noble title. Keeping "her duty" to her children in mind, she ended her relationship with Beethoven in 1805.

Countess Therese von Brunswick was another cousin of Giulietta Guicciardi as well as Beethoven's student. She was a member of the nobility in her native Hungary. Some scholars believe Beethoven dedicated his Piano Sonata No. 24 in F-sharp Major (op. 78) to her.

In 1809, Bettina Brentano returned to Vienna, the city of her birth. She remained there for three years and developed a close relationship with Beethoven, but in 1811 she married Achim von Arnim, the renowned Romantic poet. The singer Amalie Sebald nursed the

composer through an illness, but the relationship eventually became a simple friendship. In 1812 he wrote to her, "I am already better. If you think it *becoming* to pay me a visit alone, I should be delighted; but if you find it *unbecoming*, you know how I honour the freedom of all men; and however you may act in this or any other case, according to your principles or your caprice, you will always find me well-disposed and your friend."

When Beethoven was 40 he fell in love with 18-year-old Therese Malfatti, the daughter of one of his physicians. The composer may have had plans to marry this young woman, but her family opposed the idea. Some believe the Bagatelle no. 25 in A Minor, a short piano piece known as *Für Elise*, was dedicated to her. Finally, the composer tried to accept the idea that he would have to live alone and would probably never marry.

6

HEROIC METHODS

*"I am not satisfied with the work I have done so far.
From now on I intend to take a new way."*
—Ludwig van Beethoven

ETURNING FROM HEILIGENSTADT to Vienna, Beethoven began to compose. He was often so wrapped up in his work that he forgot to eat. His habit of writing notes to himself increased. Instead of scribbling on individual pieces of paper, which he tended to misplace, he now carried a notebook at all times. This helped him to organize his thoughts, review his progress, and plan in a more orderly way. Sometimes Beethoven bought pre-made sketchbooks of musical notepaper, but sometimes he stitched his own together.

In 1802, soon after Beethoven's return, he started working on the music that came to define his middle or "heroic" period. During this 10-year period many of his compositions,

🌲 Portrait of Ludwig van Beethoven, date unknown.
Library of Congress LC-USZ62-29499

such as his third symphony, the *Eroica*, and his only opera, *Fidelio*, contained heroic subjects. Beethoven's musical style changed noticeably in this middle period as he tried different musical forms, including an oratorio, and brought new approaches to his compositions.

Finding his own style, Beethoven ignored the standards that had been established by previous composers. He wrote music that suited his own idea of what a piece should include. His innovations sometimes confused audience members and critics, but most people enjoyed what they heard.

Musical Styles and Eras

Over the centuries many styles of Western classical music have changed. Composers' works are affected by the tastes, the national culture, the history, and the society in which they live. During the Renaissance, from 1450 to 1600, most music was written for religious purposes. **Gregorian chant**, used in church, had only a melodic line without **harmony** (the sounding of two or more tones simultaneously). Nonreligious music was composed for songs known as "madrigals" and some dances. Because a system of music notation did not exist, most of these pieces have not survived.

The Baroque era began in about 1600 and lasted until 1750. The word "baroque" means "elaborate"—the style of art and architecture during this period was highly decorative and ornate. Baroque music featured a continu-ous bass—a bass part that continued through the entire piece—and counterpoint, which combined two or more melodies at the same time. In this era composers wrote nonreligious music that entertained people. Opera was created and became a new musical **genre**. New instruments were fashioned and older instruments were improved.

The Classical era in music, which began in about 1750 and lasted until about 1830, moved away from elaborate ornamentation and toward balance, order, and structure. Full chords harmonized a single melody. Large instrumental music genres, like the symphony, were the fashion. The orchestra grew as the clarinet and brass instruments were developed. The piano replaced the harpsichord. Opera composers fused their music with the words.

By the **Romantic era** (music of the early 1800s until about 1900) human emotions replaced the order sought by the Classical period. Audiences wanted dramatic works. Music reflected cultural and national differences, and free-form genres, like the **nocturne**, were popular. The orchestra was further expanded as composers sought a greater range of sound.

Modern classical music since about 1900 includes some of these traditions while experimenting with the electronic means that are now available. Today's music is not always harmonious and often does not use the usual musical instruments but instead employs computers, tape recorders, and electronic instruments. It is innovative and often disregards the rules of the past.

Sew Your Own Notebook

MAKING YOUR own notebook out of scrap paper is the green thing to do. You can use it, like Beethoven and many other artists, to track your ideas and progress in a favorite endeavor or hobby, to make sketches, and jot down observations and thoughts.

You'll Need

- 20 sheets of scrap paper with at least one side blank, such as old homework pages, junk mail, invitations, used printer paper, and so on
- Scissors
- Cutting mat
- 2 large clips
- Ruler
- Pencil
- Pushpin
- Thick sewing needle
- Heavy-duty cotton thread
- Glue

1. Cut the pieces of scrap paper so that they are all the same length and width.

2. Stack the papers together on the cutting mat, making certain that they are all in an even line.

3. Clip the papers firmly together at the top and bottom.

4. Using the ruler, draw a vertical line ½ inch in from the left edge of the paper, and then mark off each inch down the line.

5. To plan your stitch holes, begin at the second inch from the top and mark each ¼ inch until one inch from the bottom.

6. Use the pushpin to poke a hole through the papers at each ¼-inch marking.

7. Thread your needle; make a knot of the loose ends so that the thread will stay in place. Stitch your papers together with the threaded needle going up through one hole and down the next one, making sure that each hole has been sewn.

8. When you complete the stitching, cut the thread, leaving enough to tie it into a knot.

9. Apply a dab of the glue to the knot.

His music also made great demands on the skills and musicianship of the orchestra members. Beethoven kept focused on his work and composed a huge amount of music during this middle period—one masterpiece after another. These works caused Beethoven to become recognized as the leading composer of his time.

Carl Czerny

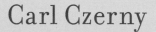

The composer and pianist Carl Czerny was born in Vienna in 1791. His family was Czech in origin. His father, Wenzel Czerny, was an oboist, organist, and pianist as well as a piano teacher, and early on he realized that his son had a wonderful gift. The boy took his first piano lessons with his father before going to study with more well-known pianists including Antonio Salieri and Beethoven. Carl was composing music at the age of seven, and by the time he was nine, he was making public appearances and was hailed as a child prodigy.

Carl Czerny's violin teacher, Wenzel Krumpholz, brought the boy to his first meeting with Beethoven. After being accepted as Beethoven's pupil, Czerny began to seriously examine and study the works of his teacher. Soon he became famous for his interpretation of Beethoven's music— the way he understood and presented how Beethoven actually wanted his compositions performed. Beethoven was pleased to find someone with such insight into his works and such a superb ability to perform them. A few years later Czerny organized a weekly series of concerts devoted to Beethoven's compositions. These concerts affirmed his reputation as an excellent interpreter of Beethoven's piano music.

At the age of 15 Czerny began giving piano lessons. As he matured he was valued as a fabulous teacher, and the wealthy families of Vienna hired him to teach their children. His pupils included the composer Franz Liszt. Although he taught many hours each day, Czerny found the time to compose and to write books of piano exercises as well as other books full of advice about how to perform Beethoven's piano music. Czerny never married. When he died, at the age of 66, he left his estate to many charities.

A New Student

DESPITE HIS intense focus on his own music in the early 1800s, Beethoven found time to mentor others. Carl Czerny, a child prodigy, was only 10 years old in 1801 when he was introduced to Beethoven. During the meeting the youngster brilliantly performed a Mozart concerto and Beethoven's Piano Sonata no. 8 in C Minor (op. 13), which the publisher had named the *Pathétique* Sonata. The composer was so impressed by the boy's talent that he offered to teach the promising pianist.

In 1842, many years after this initial visit, Czerny gave a detailed and interesting description of his first encounter with Beethoven. He described the room in Beethoven's third-floor apartment containing the piano as having bare walls and shaky chairs. Further, he noted that the home was in complete disorder with clothing, books, dirty dishes, and papers piled up everywhere. Beethoven was wearing a dark morning coat and gray trousers and had apparently not shaved for days. Czerny wrote that the composer's ears were stuffed with pieces of cotton that contained some yellow-colored medicine.

When he was a teen, Czerny began arranging some of Beethoven's orchestral works for the piano. Over the years, Beethoven and Czerny became close friends. They had much in common and respected each other enormously.

The Rise of Napoléon Bonaparte

BEETHOVEN'S DEEP passion for liberty, freedom, and the rights of all people was stirred by the writings of the Enlightenment philosophers, but he was even more influenced by the ideals of the French Revolution. At first, Beethoven was pleased with the rise of Napoléon Bonaparte, whom he pictured as a hero—a fighter for freedom and a champion of the common people.

Napoléon's plans for equality and justice led to the reform of French law and the establishment of the rules known as the Code Napoléon in 1804. Under this legal code the nobility lost its privileges and French citizens were granted their civil rights. These more fair and evenhanded laws inspired the composer.

Napoléon had led the French army in many battles. When he returned to France after a victory in Egypt, he was very famous. In 1799 he engineered an overthrow of the government and made certain that he was installed to lead the new government as its first consul. Soon after he

Get Inspired to Create Music

THINGS THAT excite you may inspire you to create something, such as a painting, a poem, or a piece of music. The idea of Napoléon bringing the right to live in freedom to all people inspired Beethoven. What inspires you?

You'll Need

∞ Musical instrument (or your voice)

∞ Pencil

∞ Music notepaper or tape recorder

1. Form a mental image of something that inspires you. It may be an idea, a person, or even a scene. You can express how the image of this inspiration makes you feel in music.

2. Think: how does this image make you feel?

Happy? Sad? Thoughtful? Angry? Joyous?

3. Try to match this feeling with a melody that you believe gives it expression.

4. Hum the melody into a tape recorder or play it on your instrument a few times.

5. This melody is the beginning of your composition; it sets up the mood. You can add to it, harmonize it, vary it, and enhance it to tell the story of what inspired you.

6. If you know music notation, you can write the melody down on the music notepaper.

7. Enjoy your creation!

gained control over France, it was announced that his Code Napoléon was now the law of France. Napoléon planned to eventually install these laws in every country in Europe that he intended to conquer.

Beethoven was confident that Napoléon would defend the principles of the French Revolution:

Napoléon Bonaparte

Napoléon Bonaparte was born in 1769 on the mountainous island of Corsica, located in the Mediterranean Sea west of Italy and southeast of France. Revolutionary fever was at its height in Europe when Napoléon was a teen living there. He attended military schools before entering the army, where he was noticed for his leadership abilities. By 1793, Napoléon had achieved the rank of brigadier general. In 1796 he was given command of the French army in Italy. He married a few days before leaving for the French conflict against Italy. After winning several major battles, Napoléon returned to France as a hero.

In 1798, Napoléon led a campaign in Egypt, where his army was cut off from its supplies by the British. Napoléon decided to return to France, where he participated in an overthrow of the government and seized power. From 1799 to 1804 Napoléon worked to modernize France. A new code of law called the Code Napoléon abolished serfdom, provided people with the right to worship as they chose, and reformed the French legal system by assuring all French citizens equality before the law.

In 1804, Napoléon had himself proclaimed emperor of France. When the French army began to defeat Austria, Francis II dissolved the Holy Roman Empire. In 1806, Austria gave up its control over Germany and Italy. Napoléon divorced his wife, Josephine, and married an Austrian princess in an effort to bind the two countries together. The French army suffered when its invasion of Russia did not go as planned, and the armies of Russia, Prussia, Britain, and Spain further weakened Napoléon's forces. In 1814, Napoléon was forced to abdicate his throne and was sent to the Island of Elba in exile. In 1815, Napoléon returned to France and rebuilt his army but was defeated at Waterloo. He was exiled to the island of St. Helena, where he died in 1821.

✻ Napoléon postage stamp. Dreamstime

liberty, equality, and brotherhood. The composer was sure that this remarkable leader would carry the spirit and idea of freedom to the people existing under the power and control of absolute rulers in the rest of Europe.

The Eroica!

BEETHOVEN WAS very pleased with the Code Napoléon and believed it proved that Napoléon cared about human rights. In 1803 the composer had planned to dedicate his Symphony no. 3 in E-flat Major (op. 55) to this champion of liberty. But a year later, when Beethoven learned that Napoléon had proclaimed himself emperor of France, he was shocked. Why would Napoléon, a supposed defender of freedom, need to claim such a title?

"So he too is nothing more than an ordinary man," the angry composer exclaimed. "Now he will trample on all human rights and indulge only in his own ambition. He will place himself above everyone and become a tyrant."

Full of anger, Beethoven stormed across the room and over to the table that held the manuscript of his Third Symphony. He grabbed the first page, which read "Bonaparte," and erased the title with a hand so heavy he left a hole in the paper. Beethoven then threw the page on the floor. The work was later published as the *Eroica,* the Italian word for "heroic."

The Third Symphony was given a private performance in the palace of Prince Lobkowitz during the summer before it was presented to the public. The premiere took place in the Theater an der Wien on April 7, 1805. As the audience glanced at the printed program, many were surprised to learn that the symphony was now dedicated to one of Beethoven's patrons, Prince Lobkowitz.

Beethoven prepared to conduct his symphony knowing that many hearing it for the first time

Music Notes: What Is a Musical Key?

A musical key is based on the basic musical building block called a "scale," which is a sequence of seven notes or pitches in ascending (going up) and descending (going down) order. The first note identifies the name of the scale, which may be major or minor depending on the notes specified in the scale. A key is the major or minor scale around which a piece of music revolves. There are 12 major scales, which create 12 major keys. There are also 12 minor scales, which form 12 minor keys. For example, a piece composed using the seven notes C, D, E, F, G, A, and B (which are the notes in the C major scale) is written in the key of C major.

Composers select a key for a piece because that particular key best expresses how they hear the music in their own minds, and they believe that it is the correct key for the range of instruments that will be performing the music. The key is an important factor in the unity of a piece. Composers also consider the contrasts and tensions that can be created between the keys that add to the variety of the music in the work. A progression made from the home key to a contrasting key adds excitement and interest to the music.

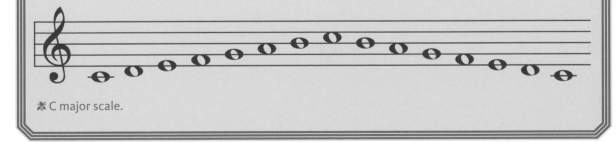

🎵 C major scale.

🎵 Napoléon Bonaparte. Dreamstime

63

Discover the Key

THE SYMPHONY no. 3 in E-flat Major (op. 55) was written in the key of E-flat major. Musicians need to know the key in which a musical score is written so that they know which notes are to be played as **sharps** and **flats**. Sharps ♯ raise the pitch of a note while flats ♭ lower the pitch of a note. The key signature located on the staff at the beginning of each composition shows the sharps or flats included in the work. For example, the following is the key signature of A major or its relative F-sharp minor:

※ A major or F-sharp minor.

To identify which key that a piece of music was written in, you can use a diagram called the "circle of fifths" that displays the keys with their sharp and flat signatures. The diagram helps musicians understand the keys used in music, key relationships, and chord relationships. The circle of fifths displays the keys in order of how many sharps or flats are found in a key. It also tells you which keys are related to each other in the chromatic scale (the 12-note scale that divides the octave into its semitones).

※ Chromatic scale.

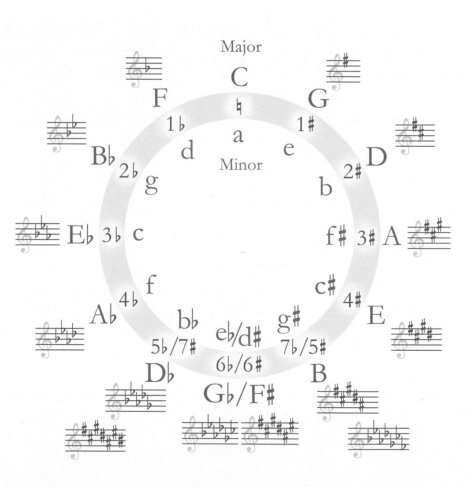

※ Circle of fifths.

The chart begins with the key of C, which has no sharps or flats. The intervals between the keys on the chart are fifths; reading clockwise, G is the fifth note away from C on the C major scale.

If you play an instrument or sing, it's useful to memorize the circle of fifths chart so you know the key of the music and the notes that are in each key.

C   G

🎵 C major scale.

You'll Need

∞ Sheet music of your favorite Beethoven composition; can be downloaded for free at the website of the International Music Score Library Project: http://imslp.org

1. Note the key signature located on the staff at the beginning of the composition you have chosen.

2. Find the same key signature on the chart.

∞ What key is indicated by the key signature?

∞ How many notes are to be played as sharps or flats?

∞ Which notes are to be played as sharps or flats?

3. To learn even more from the chart, look to see:

∞ Which scale is related to the major or minor scale that is indicated by the key signature?

The chart tells you that the most closely related key to C major is A minor, since they have the same key signature (no sharps and no flats). The next most closely related key to C major would be G major (or E minor), with one sharp, and F major (or D minor), with only one flat.

would find reasons to disapprove of and criticize this new work. This debut would make the public realize that his music had taken a new path.

First of all, he knew the *Eroica* was much longer than any other symphony that had been written in the past. He thought the audience would quickly sense that just the first movement was longer than the totality of any of Haydn's symphonies. What would the old master have said about that? Beethoven also was concerned about how the lis-

The Mannheim Orchestra

During the **Renaissance era**, court orchestras were maintained to provide entertainment for the nobility. These orchestras were small instrumental ensembles that varied in size. Since there were no standards for which instruments would be included, the sound was different for each ensemble.

By the Baroque era, orchestras were made up mainly of stringed instruments with some woodwinds including the flute and oboe. Still, the sound varied according to the size and instrumental makeup of the orchestra, which often depended on which musicians were available.

By the end of the 18th century, the instruments included in an orchestra became standardized. The major orchestras in the courts and theaters contained the same or similar instruments. Composers began to indicate which specific instruments were to perform in their works.

The Mannheim Orchestra, the most famous German orchestra of its time, took a novel approach to the presentation of music and set high standards for the orchestra. Founded in 1743, this 50-member orchestra became the model for other orchestras. It introduced new techniques and orchestral effects. Under the direction of composer and conductor Johann Stamitz, the orchestra developed into the first modern symphony orchestra. Stamitz required the musicians to attend rehearsals and be well prepared. He demanded excellence and attention to detail.

The orchestra was known for its innovative use of sound, called "dynamics," in music. Previously, the sounds an orchestra made were either loud or soft. Two innovations that were developed by the Mannheim Orchestra are known as the Mannheim **crescendo**, which increased the volume of the music, and the Mannheim rocket, a rapidly upward-moving passage. The professionalism of the Mannheim Orchestra had a tremendous influence on the improvement of the symphony orchestra.

teners would react to the raw emotional power of the *Eroica* and to his inclusion of French horns, an instrument that had never before been used in a symphony orchestra.

After the concert, reviews were mixed. Some people proclaimed the Third Symphony was a masterpiece, others were not so sure about the work. One critic suggested shortening the symphony because he believed "it would gain immensely." Another reviewer called it "daring." Some noted that they thought the piece was full of confusion. Beethoven considered what his critics wrote, but he was sure that this symphony would eventually be understood and appreciated by the public. Years later, when asked by a friend which of his symphonies was his favorite, the composer quickly responded, "Why, the *Eroica*!"

✿ French horn. Dreamstime

7

FIDELIO

"This opera will win for me the martyr's crown."
—LUDWIG VAN BEETHOVEN

IN ADDITION TO forging a new path in his orchestral compositions, Beethoven tried new genres during his middle period. In 1803 the manager of Vienna's famous Theater an der Wien asked Beethoven to write an opera that would be performed in the theater. Besides offering a salary, the manager had sweetened his proposal to Beethoven by providing him free rooms to live in at the theater while the composer was working on the opera. Beethoven liked this arrangement and accepted it gladly.

During the 19th century, opera had become very popular in Europe, and Beethoven had wanted to compose one for a long time. This proved to be a difficult project for him for many reasons. He was mainly an instrumental composer, and there were no well-established German opera traditions that he could use as a guide. He reminded himself that he had

A scene from *Fidelio*. Reproduced with permission of the Ira F. Brilliant Center for Beethoven Studies, San José State University

played the viola in the court orchestra in Bonn—there he had become familiar with a variety of operas. He had learned much about composing for the voice when he had studied with Antonio Salieri, the director of the Vienna Opera. Perhaps

---

The Beginnings of Opera

Opera was created in the late 1500s in Florence, Italy, where a group of scholars called the Florentine Camerata met to talk about the arts and sciences. It was the era called the Renaissance, meaning "rebirth," because there was a renewed interest in learning. The members of the Camerata sought to expand their knowledge.

The Florentine Camerata studied ancient Greek plays. The scholars believed that the Greeks had not spoken the words of their tragedies but had used song to perform the dramas. Unhappy with the direction taken by drama and music during the Renaissance, this collection of thinkers was determined to go back to the Greek style of presenting plays. They studied the works of the ancient philosophers to learn what they had to say about the nature of Greek drama and decided to experiment. Out of

this experiment emerged a new art form: opera.

The members of the Florentine Camerata wrote several operas, but the first work considered by scholars to be a true opera was *L'Orfeo, favola in musica* (Orpheus, a Legend in Music) by Claudio Monteverdi in 1607. *L'Orfeo* contains all of the elements of a proper opera: singing and acting, orchestra accompaniment, scenery, costumes, and dance. Although at first opera was only performed for the courts, its popularity grew, and soon it became grand entertainment for the public. The dramatic music, ornate costumes, vivid scenery, and many special effects employed during an opera attracted many admirers. By the end of the 17th century this new art form had flourished throughout Europe and opera houses were constructed in most major European cities.

---

such an undertaking would be a challenge, but it could be done.

He just had to find the right **libretto** (the text of an opera or oratorio). Beethoven had looked for a good text to put to music for many years. Never finding what he wanted, he wrote to a friend, "Always the same old story: the Germans can not put together a good libretto." In another letter, sent to Gerhard von Breuning, the composer had more to say about this frustrating situation: "I need a text which stimulates me; it must be something moral, uplifting. Texts such as Mozart composed I should never have been able to set to music. I could never have got myself into a mood for immoral texts. I have received many librettos, but, as I have said, none that met my wishes."

Tales of Rescue

AFTER THE French Revolution, "rescue operas" depicting loyalty, devotion, and bravery in dangerous situations were greatly admired by the public. In a time of war and revolution this type of plot, in which good overcomes evil and the hero or heroine escapes from certain death, was well liked by the audiences attending operas.

Beethoven had never found the "right story" to set to music until the German librettist Joseph Sonnleithner brought to his attention a French libretto written by Jean-Nicolas Bouilly. It was the

🎵 A scene from *Fidelio*. Reproduced with permission of the Ira F. Brilliant Center for Beethoven Studies, San José State University

story of Florestan, a wrongfully imprisoned man who is rescued from this injustice by his loyal wife, Leonore. The story excited the composer. When Beethoven was told that this tale was based on real events that had taken place during the French Revolution, he knew he had finally found what he had been seeking for so many years. The plot of the story emphasizes the importance of

Women in Music in the 1800s

In Beethoven's day women had a restricted role outside of their homes. Not many were able to overcome these restrictions and gain respect for their abilities as musicians. But some talented women were able to pursue the arts and enjoy limited careers.

Born in Hamburg, Germany, in 1805, Fanny Mendelssohn Hensel was the sister of the composer Felix Mendelssohn. She wrote piano pieces and songs. Although she was very talented her family did not encourage her to continue composing once she reached adulthood, but she persisted. In a letter to her brother she wrote: "Since I know in advance that you won't be pleased, I'll go about this awkwardly. Laugh at me, if you like, but at the age of forty I'm as afraid of my brother as I was of Father when I was fourteen. . . . In a word I'm beginning to publish."

Clara Wieck Schumann, born in 1819, was giving public concerts by the age of 12. She published several pieces for the piano before her marriage to the composer Robert Schumann. As she grew older she lost her confidence in a woman's right to have a career, stating, "A woman must not desire to compose—there has never yet been one able to do it." Raising a large family and running her household consumed much of her time, but she was able to perform many of her husband's compositions in concert. When Robert Schumann passed away, his widow taught music and continued to perform in public. Today her compositions are often performed and recorded.

The French composer Louise Dumont Farrenc was well known during her lifetime. Born in Paris in 1804, she had the opportunity to study at the famous French Conservatory of Music, where, in 1842, she became the only 19th-century woman the school hired as a professor. Farrenc drew large audiences at her concert tours, and her own compositions were heard in many concert halls.

The Baroness Dorothea von Ertmann was born in 1781 in Frankfurt, Germany. She had a gift for interpreting Beethoven's music and was the first pianist to perform all of his sonatas. Beethoven was a great admirer of her talent and dedicated his Piano Sonata in A Major (op. 101) to her.

fairness, loyalty, and freedom—the lofty ideals that Beethoven held sacred.

First titled after the name of the heroine, "Leonore," but eventually changed to *Fidelio*, the opera was translated from the French and rewritten into German by Joseph Sonnleithner. Beethoven began working to set the libretto to music. As always, he completely wrapped himself into the work. Beethoven lingered over every note, considering every possibility, as he labored on the score. He noticed that the story contained little action but included a great deal of emotion.

The main character Leonore, wife of a nobleman, was exactly the type of woman who appealed to the composer. Beethoven had high ideals of what a "perfect" woman should be—his mother had set the high example for him. He fondly remembered her as a gentle, religious, moral, and virtuous woman. Beethoven wrote, "From childhood on, I learned to love virtue."

Fidelio is set in Spain in the late 1700s. The evil prison warden, Don Pizzaro, has secretly imprisoned his enemy, the Spanish nobleman Florestan, and plans to murder him. Beethoven was intrigued by the idea that brave Leonore would risk her own life to try to rescue her husband. In order to accomplish this Leonore disguises herself as a man she names "Fidelio," evoking the image of loyalty and devotion. Cloaked in the clothes of a man, she befriends the jailer and offers to work for him so that she can enter the prison. Standing on the staircase leading down to the dark stone dungeon, she sees a man in a cell and thinks it may be her husband. When the man speaks, even with a single oil lamp burning, Fidelio can tell it certainly is Florestan.

Don Pizzaro knows that a minister is being sent by the king to check on rumors that he has committed criminal offenses. Pizzaro realizes that he must get rid of the wrongly imprisoned man before the minister arrives. He tries to convince the jailer to commit the murder, but the jailer refuses, and the warden decides to kill Florestan himself. Soon Don Pizzaro descends into the dungeon to murder the prisoner, but Leonore places herself between the two men, daring the villain to "kill the wife first."

By the conclusion of the opera, Leonore has saved her husband's life and the bewildered Don Pizzaro is led away in chains and sent to prison by the king's minister. The prisoners and townspeople gather and sing "Hail to the Day" as Leonore and Florestan embrace. All is well; Florestan is rescued.

During rehearsals for the opera, Beethoven quarreled with the singers, who insisted that the **arias** (a song performed by a single voice) were impossible to sing. He also argued with the conductor, Ignaz von Seyfried, and the members of the orchestra because he was convinced that they were purposely ignoring his directions. Writing

Create a Diorama Picturing the Dungeon Scene in Fidelio

A DIORAMA is a small model that depicts a scene, such as the dungeon scene in *Fidelio* in which Leonore stands up to Don Pizzaro. Create this scene using a cardboard box as the "stage." Work from the back of the box to the front. Keep your objects and figures in scale relative to the size of the box. Larger objects should be placed farther back.

You'll Need

∞ Scrap paper
∞ Pencil
∞ Ruler
∞ Sturdy shoebox or larger cardboard box
∞ Scissors
∞ Small objects to serve as "props" for your scene, such as a chain, a dollhouse-sized bench, and so on
∞ Figures of the main characters Leonore, Don Pizzaro, and Florestan drawn, cut out of a magazine, or made out of clay
∞ Light pieces of cardboard to anchor pictures, if needed
∞ Black construction paper
∞ 10 small stones of various sizes and shapes
∞ Glue

1. Decide on the scale of your diorama, such as one foot equals one inch. So, a five-foot-tall woman would be five inches tall, a three-foot chair would be three inches, and so on.

2. Plan your diorama on the scrap paper.

3. Collect your materials and props, including the small stones.

4. Create figures of the characters. Make any paper figures with tabs on the bottom so that they can be glued to the box. If the pictures do not stand up by themselves, cut out and glue small cardboard holders with bottom tabs to the back of the pictures.

5. Cut the black construction paper to fit the back, sides, and bottom of the box. Glue the construction paper to the insides of the box.

6. Place your objects and figures, moving them until you are satisfied.

7. Glue the objects and figures securely in place.

8. Apply glue to the small stones and place them in the box to represent the stones of the dungeon.

9. Let the glue dry thoroughly before moving the diorama.

to a friend only two days before the debut, Beethoven expressed his annoyance: "Pray to persuade Seyfried to conduct my opera today as I wish to see and hear it from a distance; in this way at least my patience will not be so severely tried by the rehearsal as when I am close enough to hear my music bungled."

The rehearsals were difficult and long. Beethoven was expecting a great deal from the performers. He was sure that they were fighting him at every turn, and he left the rehearsals frustrated, drained, and angry.

Opening During an Invasion

ONE WEEK before *Fidelio* opened, Napoléon's troops marched into Vienna. The French and the British were at war again. France wanted to control Europe. In 1805 it appeared that Napoléon planned to invade Britain. He paraded his French soldiers along the shore of the channel that separated the two countries. Shocking everyone expecting a battle between France and England, Napoléon suddenly turned his army around and rapidly marched them away from the English Channel and into Europe.

Austria and Russia had formed an alliance with Britain against Napoléon. Their soldiers were

The *Triumph of Napoléon* is engraved on a portion of the Arc de Triomphe in Paris. Dreamstime

spread across the continent of Europe waiting for the signal to move forward when the French army had reached the shores of Britain. Always a great military thinker, Napoléon had seen a flaw in the strategy of the allies and used it to defeat them. Within six weeks, the French had reached the shores of the Danube River. Catching the Austrian army by surprise, Napoléon's army surrounded the soldiers at the town of Ulm, located on the Danube, causing the Austrian military to quickly surrender.

Soon after the Austrian defeat at Ulm, the victorious French army streamed into Vienna. Fearing the worst, the Austrian aristocrats fled in advance of the invading French army. Even the emperor left the city. One evening Beethoven was sitting with some friends in his favorite coffeehouse when a French officer passed by. Shaking his fist

⚔ A scene depicting the Austrian surrender at Ulm by sculptor Pierre Cartellier. Photograph by Marie-Lan Nguyen

at the officer, Beethoven yelled, "If I as a general knew as much about strategy as I the composer know about counterpoint I would give you something to do!" One of his friends quickly yanked down Beethoven's arm. Afraid that the French soldier would respond to this angry comment with force he whispered to Beethoven, "Fortunately, the officer has kept on walking. You must learn not to yell at someone with a rifle."

On the evening of *Fidelio*'s first performance, the audience was filled with French soldiers instead of the usual operagoers, who had escaped Vienna in an attempt to get away from the invading French army. The soldiers came to the Theater an der Wien looking for an evening's entertainment, but they did not know what to expect to see in the theater that night. Since the French soldiers did not understand German and perhaps were not exactly the type of people who enjoyed fine music, they did not appreciate the opera. Their response to the work was cold and distant— there was hardly any of the usual applause. The following night the theater was practically empty. The regular Viennese audience was gone, and the French soldiers had chosen not to attend the next performance. Beethoven was very disheartened by this situation, and his anger toward Napoléon increased.

Even the few critics and regular opera attendees who had seen the work let the composer know that *Fidelio* was not yet right. Beethoven was prepared to rewrite, revise, rework, and recompose. He thoroughly inspected and examined every aspect of the work. Always wanting his music to express exactly what he wanted the audience to hear and understand, he changed one of Florestan's arias 18 times before he was satisfied with it.

A new librettist now worked on the text. He was Beethoven's old friend from Bonn and former pupil, Stephan von Breuning. Another **overture** was written, and the work was shortened into two acts from the original three. The second premiere of the altered *Fidelio* took place in 1806. It was more of a success than its debut had been in 1805 but still not a huge hit with the audience or the critics.

Right after the second debut, Beethoven got involved in an argument with the management of the theater and promptly withdrew the opera from any further performances. *Fidelio* would have to wait a number of years for its next review, alteration, and presentation.

Beethoven's fiery temper led him to another argument, this time with his longtime patron Prince Lichnowsky. In October 1806 the prince requested a concert to be held in his mansion but did not tell Beethoven that he would have some of Napoléon's military officers in attendance. The officers had hidden in a room behind the ballroom where the concert was to take place.

When Beethoven entered the house he quickly observed the officers, whose presence made him furious. He hurriedly left the mansion without giving the concert. He wrote to Prince Lichnowsky: "Prince, what you are, you are by accident of birth; what I am, I am of myself. There are and will be thousands of princes. There is only one Beethoven."

The Fifth and Sixth Symphonies

AFTER HIS disappointing experience with *Fidelio*, the composer decided to give up on opera for a while and put the score on a shelf. He kept himself busy writing instrumental music exclusively. In 1808, at age 38 he completed Symphony no. 5 in C Minor (op. 67) with its distinctive motif.

A motif is a melodic/rhythmic unit that is a major building block of a work and is often repeated throughout a piece of music. The motif that opens the Fifth Symphony is varied throughout the piece and also ends it. Described as "three shorts and a long"—bum bum bum BUUUUUUUMMMM—this motif dominates the symphony and is recognized around the world today. It has been said that when he was asked what the opening motif of the Fifth Symphony symbolizes, Beethoven replied, "Thus Fate knocks at the door."

🎵 Fifth Symphony motif. *Courtesy of Susan Silberman*

Music Notes: What Is a Motif?

A motif is a rhythmic, harmonic, or melodic pattern in a piece of music. It can be of any length, but normally, a motif is a short idea and may be only a few notes long. The motif is a building block on which the structure of the piece is built and can be recognized throughout the composition. The word comes from the Latin *motus*, which means "to move." Sometimes a motif is called a "theme"; the words are interchangeable.

Composers use a motif to present and then develop a musical idea. Some opera composers use a motif to stand for a person, an idea, an object, or a place. Renaissance composers used a motif that was repeated and echoed by several voices in counterpoint.

The operatic composer Richard Wagner used a system of musical themes that he called "leitmotifs" to suggest characters, ideas, geographical settings, and even objects.

The brief motif that Beethoven employed in his Symphony no. 5 in C Minor, op. 67 is one of the best examples of the use of a motif. In just a few notes Beethoven presented a musical idea that is remarkable and memorable. Around this single motif he was able to construct a magnificent symphony.

The Fifth Symphony contains many other unique and unexpected elements. It has two movements that are joined together and reuses an earlier theme in the finale. It was also the first symphony to include trombones. But, most unusual for its time, the single—now famous—motif unifies the entire piece.

During his stay in Heiligenstadt, Beethoven had made sketches for his Symphony no. 6 in F Major (op. 68), which he called the "Pastoral Symphony, or Recollections of Country Life." The Sixth Symphony is one of two that the composer gave a name besides a number. He did title the Third Symphony as the *Eroica* as well. Usually his publishers, friends, or critics offered their own names for his works.

In his notes for the Sixth Symphony, Beethoven mentioned how much he loved nature. Nothing made him feel better than a stroll through the countryside. A bubbling brook or a bird singing high in a tree inspired and pleased him. His letters often declared how important being able to enjoy and experience nature was to him. In 1810, Beethoven wrote to a friend, "How delighted I will be to ramble for awhile through the bushes, woods, under trees, through grass and around rocks. No one can love the country as much as I do. For surely woods, trees and rocks produce the echo that man desires to hear."

Beethoven often vacationed away from Vienna and chose to go to various resort towns during the spring and summer. These trips away from a sweltering and muggy place and into the breezy countryside during the warmer months refreshed him and raised his spirits. Staying in small communities and villages, far from the crowded and noisy city, often provided him with musical ideas.

In the first drafts of the Sixth Symphony Beethoven wrote the comment: "The hearer should be permitted to discover the situations for himself." He wanted listeners to be able to find and hear the sounds of nature in the work. Beethoven took this idea one step farther when he wrote in the concert program notes that the *Pastoral* contained "more an expression of feeling than painting."

The Fifth and Sixth Symphonies debuted at the same concert, held at the Theater an der Wien with Beethoven conducting. The concert included other works besides the two symphonies and lasted over four hours. It was exhausting for the musicians and quite lengthy for the audience, but most of the people remained in their seats for the entire performance.

Fidelio *Reprised*

EIGHT YEARS after the second debut of *Fidelio*, Beethoven, with Georg Friedrich Treitschke, a new librettist, would resume his work on the opera. A new overture was composed and the libretto reworked. The improvements were much more dramatic in this third, final version, which premiered at the Kärntnertortheater in Vienna

Picture the Music

MUSIC STIRS up images, like paintings, in our minds. Beethoven's *Pastoral* Symphony is classified as **program music**, which purposely intends to evoke mental images by creating a scene in music. Beethoven allowed the music to suggest feelings rather than trying to paint a specific picture. Let your imagination wander through the mental images that the symphony creates while you listen to it, then draw those images on paper.

You'll Need

∞ CD or MP3 download of the first two movements of Symphony no. 6 in F Major (op. 68), the *Pastoral* Symphony

∞ Music-listening device (such as an iPod, computer, or CD player)

∞ Sketchbook paper

∞ Pastels, crayons, or markers

1. The first movement is entitled "Awakening of Cheerful Feelings Upon Arriving in the Country." It describes Beethoven's feelings on arriving in the countryside.

2. Pay attention and try to identify the seven motifs that appear in this first movement. Close your eyes, let your mind wander, and let the images flow.

3. What does the music cause you to see? Draw your images.

4. The second movement is entitled "By the Brook." What does the opening played by the strings sound like to you? Draw it.

5. Beethoven identified the birdcalls played by the woodwinds in this movement as the nightingale (flute), the quail (oboe), and the cuckoo (clarinet). What image comes to your mind when hearing these sounds? Draw it.

6. Make your pictures as colorful as the symphony.

on May 23, 1814, and greatly pleased the audience. In a letter to the librettist, Treitschke, Beethoven wrote: "I could have composed something new far more quickly than patch up the old with something new, as I am now doing. This opera will win for me the martyr's crown."

This last version of *Fidelio* was considered to be a masterpiece. When the French composer Hector Berlioz saw the opera he declared, "That music sets your insides on fire."

8

Straining to Hear

*"I shall seize Fate by the throat; it shall certainly
not bend and crush me completely."*

—Ludwig van Beethoven, in a letter to his friend Franz Wegeler

As the years passed it was increasingly difficult for Beethoven to hear his music. It helped somewhat that piano craftsmen were making many improvements to the instruments. They had enhanced the strength of the wooden cases with metal bars and had increased the number of octaves on the keyboards. Beethoven's heavy-handed style of playing was demanding on his pianos, which were often falling apart and in need of replacement.

The Incident at Teplice by Carl Rohling.
Beethoven Museum, Bonn

Nanette Streicher (1769–1833)

Anna Maria Stein, called by her nickname "Nanette," was the daughter of the famous organ and piano builder Johann Andreas Stein and his wife, Magdalena. Her father was also a composer and piano teacher. Nanette began her music studies with her father and developed into an excellent pianist. She and Beethoven were introduced to each other while they were still teenagers in Bonn.

After her marriage to musician and piano maker Johann Andreas Streicher, the couple moved to Vienna, where they established the Streicher piano factory. Devoted to music, they opened their home to many musicians for salon performances. In Vienna, Nanette and Beethoven resumed their friendship. She took a motherly interest in him, helping him as much as she could. Often she would go to clean up Beethoven's untidy apartment and take his clothes to be mended and cleaned. Beethoven turned to

✹ Nanette Streicher.
Courtesy of the Sophie Drinker Institute

her for all kinds of advice and valued her input. They wrote more than 60 letters to each other over the years. In one letter, dated 1817, Beethoven asks his friend to take care of some laundry for him. In these letters the composer frequently vented his complaints about his servants to her.

Johann and Nanette had a son, Johann Baptist, and a daughter, Sophie, who was also a gifted pianist. Sometimes the mother and daughter performed piano **duets** in their salons. Sophie also was concerned about Beethoven's well-being. In a letter written on December 28, 1816, the composer comments that Nanette's "dear, good daughter came to see me."

After the death of her husband, Nanette and her son ran the piano factory together. During this era when it was rare for women to have influence in business, Nanette was very involved in the planning and design of the pianos that her company built.

Beethoven asked his friend the piano maker Johann Andreas Streicher to build a piano for him that would sound as loud as possible. Streicher and his wife, Nanette, held many important and brilliant salons in their home that the composer enjoyed attending. They even commissioned a bust of Beethoven for their home. Beethoven had used several pianos built by Streicher's company, which produced instruments that were very sensitive and suited the composer's needs.

✹ Bartolomeo Cristofori, 1726.

Life at Teplice

IN 1812, Beethoven went to see his doctor. Now in his early 40s, he had not been feeling well for quite a while. The doctor advised him to spend the summer in the resort town of Teplice, located in northern Bohemia. The town, near the border between today's Germany and Czech Republic, was surrounded by mountains and beautified by many gardens. When he arrived, Beethoven spotted many lovely places for his future walks. His doctor had ordered him to bathe in the therapeutic waters located there, saying, "Hot springs have long been considered to have healing properties. Teplice is exactly the right place to make you feel better."

The countess Bettina Brentano von Arnim, one of Beethoven's friends, was also in Teplice at the time. The young woman was a writer and novelist, an amateur composer, and a singer. She had married an aristocratic novelist and poet, Ludwig Achim von Arnim. The countess also enjoyed long walks. She and Beethoven took many turns around the charming town together while talking about music and literature.

During one of these promenades the countess mentioned that her friend, the famous German writer Johann Wolfgang von Goethe, was coming to Teplice. "Would you like to meet him?" she asked with a smile, knowing how much Beethoven would relish such an opportunity. The composer had long admired Goethe.

Capturing Beethoven's Image

In 1812, Beethoven's friend Johann Streicher asked the sculptor Franz Klein to create a bust, a sculpture of the composer's shoulders and head. Streicher wanted to place busts of famous musicians around the music room in his home. First Klein made a plaster mold of Beethoven's face called a "life mask." The composer squirmed and fussed under the plaster. Never a patient man, Beethoven tired of waiting for the plaster mold to dry. He yelled to the artist that he was very uncomfortable and might be suffocating. Without waiting for a response from the sculptor, he pulled off the mask and tossed it to the floor, where it broke into two pieces. The plaster would have to be reapplied! Klein calmed Beethoven down so that they could try again. This time the composer was willing to wait until the plaster had set, and the sculptor was able to remove it from his face. This life mask is thought to be the truest likeness of Beethoven's facial features.

Life mask of Beethoven by Franz Klein, 1812. Reproduced with permission of the Ira F. Brilliant Center for Beethoven Studies, San José State University

Beethoven responded, "Goethe's poems exert a great power over me not only because of their contents but also because of their rhythms; I am stimulated to compose by this language, which builds itself up to higher orders as if through spiritual agencies, and bears in itself the secret of

Make a Plaster Life Mask

BEFORE THE age of photography, life masks were sometimes made of famous people. Beethoven had a life mask made by the artist Franz Klein. President Abraham Lincoln had two life masks fashioned, in 1860 and 1865. You can make a life mask of your friend using a few simple materials.

You'll Need

- ∞ Drop cloth
- ∞ Friend
- ∞ Smock
- ∞ Shower cap
- ∞ Petroleum jelly
- ∞ Scissors
- ∞ 2 rolls plaster gauze (available at craft stores) cut into 1-by-4-inch strips
- ∞ 1 cup water
- ∞ Crumpled paper towels to support the drying mask
- ∞ White glue
- ∞ Clear varnish

1. Place the drop cloth to protect the floor.

2. Have your friend lie down. Use the smock and shower cap to protect his or her clothes and hair.

3. Spread a thin coat of petroleum jelly on the subject's face and neck—coat the lips, hairline, eyebrows, eyelashes, and the sides of the nose. Be extra careful around the eyes.

4. Dampen a strip of gauze in the water. Gently use your fingers to remove any excess water, and place the strip diagonally from the eyebrow over the bridge of the nose.

5. Do the same with the second strip but in the opposite direction, forming an X with the two strips.

6. Place a strip across the forehead, overlapping the X.

7. Working down from the forehead, keeping the eyes and nostrils uncovered, continue to place overlapping strips to the jaw but not under the chin. Keep smoothing down the strips with your fingers as you work.

8. Repeat with a second layer, and then let the layers dry for about 10 minutes.

9. Guide the mask off by gently pulling on the outer edges.

10. Place the mask on crumpled paper towels to dry overnight.

11. Spread some white glue on the edges of your mask to make them stronger. Allow the glue to dry.

12. When the mask is completely dry protect it with a light layer of varnish.

harmonies." His answer pleased the young woman, who replied, "I will make the arrangements."

Beethoven had read Goethe's books at the University of Bonn and marveled at his poetry. He looked forward to meeting the esteemed author. The countess was true to her word and arranged their first encounter. Goethe came to visit Beethoven at his lodgings in Teplice a few times. The men were obviously impressed by each other's talents but had very different personalities, attitudes, and thoughts about politics. On one occasion these differences became very clear.

Goethe had arrived on a July afternoon. It was not a hot or humid day, and there was no sign of rain, so the men decided to take a stroll in the fresh air. Walking arm in arm, the men had just entered a beautiful park filled with colorful flower beds and tall shade trees. Goethe noticed that the empress and other members of the imperial family were approaching.

"Come, let us pay our respects to her royal highness," the poet said. Goethe respected and admired the Austrian royalty, while his companion certainly did not. Beethoven bristled at the idea of greeting and bowing to royalty. "Let us keep walking," he said. "The empress should come over to us to pay her respects, not the other way around."

Shocked at these words, Goethe stared into the eyes of the composer before he dropped his

Johann Wolfgang von Goethe

An important German writer, Johann Wolfgang von Goethe was born in Frankfurt, a city in the Holy Roman Empire. His father was a lawyer, and his mother was a daughter of the mayor of Frankfurt. Goethe's parents were concerned with giving their son the best education. His father and various tutors taught him many subjects ranging from languages to fencing.

At 16 Goethe left his home to study law at the University of Leipzig, where he began writing plays. Forced by an illness to come home three years later, he did not return to school for two years but spent his recovery reading and learning. The young man graduated in 1771 and returned to his hometown to practice law, but he did not enjoy this profession and soon returned to writing. His first novel,

published in 1774, earned him a reputation as an excellent writer. In 1775 the Duke of Weimar offered Goethe a ministerial position in his court; he remained in this job for 10 years.

His most famous work is *Faust*, a poetic drama in two parts, which tells the tale of an old man who sells his soul to the devil in return for youth, power, and knowledge. Goethe labored over this project for more than 50 years. Published after Goethe's death in 1833, *Faust* became the basis of many other works including an opera and several paintings. His writing covered many subjects ranging from scientific papers to poetry. Goethe's ideas had a tremendous influence on European literature and philosophy.

✤ Johann Wolfgang von Goethe (1749–1832) Courtesy of Marcus Kaar, portrait.kaar.at

arm. The poet removed his top hat and strode over to bow and speak to the empress. True to his principles, Beethoven made certain that his hat was in place over his thick hair and then clasped his hands behind his back before he continued on his walk. The empress and her party had to step aside to make room for him as he hurried by.

Later, when Goethe found Beethoven, the composer said to the poet, "I waited for you because I respect you and I admire your work, but you have shown too great an esteem to those people." The poet responded that he had to leave.

Apparently Goethe was quite upset by this event. In a letter to his wife he stated, "His talent astonished me" but noted that Beethoven had "an absolutely uncontrolled personality." He ended any contact with the composer after that day. A few weeks later, Beethoven wrote to his publisher, "The atmosphere at court is much to the liking of Goethe, more than a poet should."

That August, Beethoven explained his actions on that day to a friend, saying, "When two persons like Goethe and I meet, these grand folk must be made to see what our sort consider great."

Teplice was the site of another infamous aspect of Beethoven's life. While there he wrote three love letters that have created a mystery that has never been solved. These three letters are known as the "Immortal Beloved" letters. Scholars have tried to guess which woman Beethoven

♣ *The Incident at Teplice* by Carl Rohling.
Beethoven Museum, Bonn

had in mind when he wrote them, since he did not write a name to address the woman but instead called her "my immortal beloved," "my angel," and "my dearest creature." Could the letters have been written to Antonie Bretano, Therese von Brunswick, Giulietta Guicciardi, or Bettina Brentano or to someone else? These undated letters were never mailed and were found after his death in the secret compartment of Beethoven's desk.

In addition to attending to personal affairs with friends and romantic interests in the tiny spa town, Beethoven found Teplice was the perfect place for work. His notebook was crowded with ideas for his Symphony no. 7 in A Major (op. 92). He expanded the introduction of the main key in the first movement and created a second theme presented by a solo oboe. Beethoven wanted to allow the first movement to build up its intensity. For the second movement he employed a repeated rhythmic pattern. In the third movement, Beethoven decided that a scherzo and a **trio** should intertwine. The first parts of the symphony led to a last movement full of energy and dancing rhythms.

Beethoven was very pleased with this piece and looked forward to conducting its debut. When it was time to return to Vienna in the fall, he left Teplice with this symphony and his many notes for the composition of his Symphony no. 8 in F Major (op. 93).

The Defeat of Napoléon

IN JUNE 1813 the news of the defeat of Napoléon's army by the forces of the Duke of Wellington, Arthur Wellesley, reached Vienna. Beethoven was thrilled that Napoléon was finally losing

♣ A British etching celebrating the defeat of Napoléon. Library of Congress LC-DIG-ppmsca-04308

battles, and he hoped that these losses would cause the dictator's downfall and that the French would soon leave Austria. In honor of Wellington's triumph over the French at the Battle of Vitoria, Beethoven composed *Wellington's Victory* (op. 91).

⚘ The Duke of Wellington.
Courtesy of Marcus Kaar, portrait.kaar.at

The German inventor Johann Maelzel had asked the composer to write this piece, which musically re-creates the scene of the Battle of Vitoria, for an invention that he had built called the *panharmonicon*—a mechanical keyboard instrument. Happy to assist his friend and pleased to compose a piece to celebrate Wellington's success in the war, Beethoven even created special effects in the music, specifically for the *panharmonicon*, that simulated the sounds of battle.

The composer also decided to write an orchestral version of the work. It was determined that the Seventh Symphony and *Wellington's Victory* would both be premiered at a charity concert to benefit the Austrian and Bavarian soldiers who had been injured during the battles against the French army. The concert was a huge success.

The Duke of Wellington yet again led his forces against Emperor Napoléon's army at the Battle of Waterloo in 1815. This was the last battle that led to the downfall of Napoléon. Beethoven was delighted when the French tyrant was sent into exile, but he also noted that Napoléon had exported the ideals of the French Revolution to most of Europe. Beethoven knew that the common people would never allow these high ideals to wither away. Eventually reform was going to weaken the rule of the European monarchies over the people, and this pleased him. He felt Napoléon had accomplished some good things after all.

Hearing Aids

REALIZING THAT his hearing was continuing to worsen, in 1814 Beethoven asked the creative Johann Maelzel to design some ear trumpets for him. An ear trumpet is a device that captures and boosts sounds, which travel up through a tube that is held close to the ear. It is most effective if a person is speaking right into the opening. Even though these devices did not help him for long, Beethoven always carried a small ear trumpet with him.

What Caused Beethoven's Health Problems?

Beethoven consulted with many doctors as his health and hearing loss grew worse. None of them understood what was causing the problems. The physicians suggested many different treatments, such as bathing in hot springs, but they were not successful. Believing research might help others, the composer requested that an autopsy be performed after his death. This was done just one day after the composer's death in 1827, by Dr. Johann Wagner. His report stated that Beethoven's auditory nerves were damaged and that the auditory arteries were thickened, but he did not specify the cause of this damage.

Within the past 20 years, by studying his hair and bones, researchers thought they had found answers to questions about what caused the composer's illnesses, deafness, and death. In 1994 a locket containing some of Beethoven's hair, known as the Guevara Lock, was purchased at an auction and donated to the Ira F. Brilliant Center for Beethoven Studies at San José State University in California. Inspecting the hair under a microscope led researchers to conclude that DNA testing could be done on the sample.

In 2005, American scientists at a research facility in Illinois began the Beethoven Research Project using X-rays to scan bones that had been taken from Beethoven's head. The director of the project announced that large amounts of lead were found in these bones. The same results had been discovered during the DNA testing of the hair sample. However, in 2010 the Ira F. Brilliant Center for Beethoven Studies at San José State University collaborated with Dr. Andrew C. Todd, an expert in lead poisoning at the Mount Sinai School of Medicine in New York, to retest the samples. And now the mystery continues—the doctor performing the retesting concluded that the amount of lead found in Beethoven's skull fragments was about the normal amount expected in a man of his age. Therefore, the scientist declared that although the lead in his body may have caused his grumpiness, it was not the cause of the composer's death.

How Does an Ear Trumpet Work?

BEETHOVEN'S EAR trumpets were made of metal, but you can make one that uses the same concepts out of stiff paper.

You'll Need

∾ 8-by-10-inch sheet of stiff paper, such as oak tag (available at craft stores)

∾ Tape

1. Roll the paper into a cone shape, secure with tape, and set aside. This is your ear trumpet.

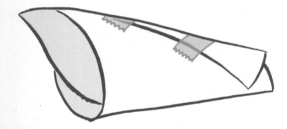

2. Listen to the sounds in the room. What do you hear? From which direction is sound coming—above or below you, behind you, or from the side?

3. Now hold the small opening of the paper cone to your ear, being careful not to stick it *into* your ear.

4. Listen to the same sounds with the ear trumpet. Is there a difference in the sounds? Does the ear trumpet help you hear?

5. Try covering up your other ear with your hand to block out sound, and test your hearing in one ear with and without the ear trumpet.

6. You can test listening to sounds in other rooms and outdoors with and without your ear trumpet. Listen to music or to someone talking. (Not too loud, though; loud sounds can damage your hearing.)

How does the ear trumpet work? Sound travels through the air as vibrations, called "sound waves." Your outer ear is pointed forward and collects these sound waves. Your outer ear also helps you tell from which direction a sound is coming. The ear trumpet works by collecting sound waves in the large part of the cone and funneling them to your ear. These sound waves make your eardrum vibrate, and this vibration is passed on to the middle ear, which contains three bones that amplify and conduct the vibrations to the inner ear. The cochlea, a small tube that is curled like a snail's shell, is in the inner ear. The cochlea contains tiny cells called "hair cells" that move when the vibrations reach them. The hair cells create an electrical signal that the auditory nerve sends to the brain.

In 1818 Beethoven began to carry around a blank-paged book in which people could write down what they wished to say to him. He had withdrawn from formal social activities but still saw his friends, and these conversation books allowed them to communicate. His visitors wrote down their questions and answers in the books, but Beethoven usually spoke to them in response, so much of the recorded exchanges are one-sided. When Beethoven died, about 400 of these books were found in his room. Once the composer accepted the fact that he could not hear, he found ways to stay connected to people and to communicate with the world.

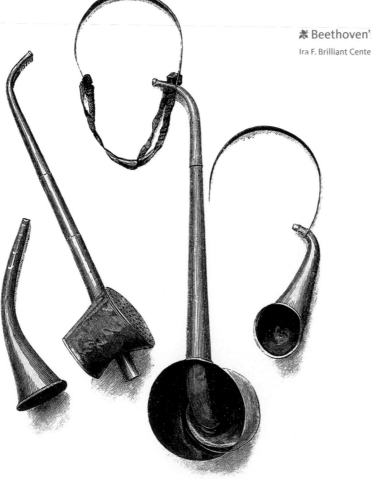

✳ Beethoven's ear trumpets. Reproduced with permission of the Ira F. Brilliant Center for Beethoven Studies, San José State University

9

DEAR KARL

"I have never thought of writing for reputation and honor. What I have in my heart must come out; that is the reason why I compose."
—LUDWIG VAN BEETHOVEN

BEETHOVEN ENCOUNTERED TROUBLES with his family throughout his life. In 1794, Caspar Carl had followed his older brother to Vienna. Although they frequently disagreed, Beethoven helped his brother financially and often sent him pupils for music lessons. By 1800, Caspar Carl had found a job as a clerk. He also often served as Beethoven's secretary, copying his scores and dealing with his publishers. But over the years the relationship between the brothers grew more tense and uneasy. This tension was caused, in part, by Caspar Carl's dishonesty when he tried to sell some of his own compositions as Beethoven's.

✼ An antique postcard shows the houses Beethoven rented during his vacations.

Another source of friction had arisen between the brothers in 1806, when Beethoven let it be known that he did not approve of his brother's new wife, Johanna. He felt she was not a woman of high morals and character. His sister-in-law, in return, harbored the same feelings of distrust and dislike toward the composer. Several months after Caspar Carl and Johanna's marriage, the couple gave birth to a baby boy, named Karl.

Beethoven's brother suffered from tuberculosis, a common lung disease in those days and the same illness that had killed their mother. When Caspar Carl realized that he was dying, he mentioned to his brother that he was considering having him share the guardianship of his young nephew, Karl, with Johanna. Beethoven was greatly concerned since he and Johanna could barely tolerate being in the same room and asked his brother to change his mind. He was certain that Johanna was not a fit mother for Karl, whom he loved and planned to treat as if he were his own son.

Caspar Carl believed that for the sake of the child, his brother had to give Johanna a chance to prove that she was a fine mother. Perhaps Caspar Carl thought that if they had to make decisions about the boy together, his wife and brother would find a way to change their feelings about each other. A short time later Beethoven learned that this joint guardianship plan had been written into Caspar Carl's will. Once again he tried to convince his brother that it was a bad idea; however,

it was too late. In November 1815, Caspar Carl passed away, and his will had not been changed. The legal document he left behind made Johanna and Beethoven equally responsible for the child, whose welfare and well-being became a foremost worry for Beethoven.

Family Battles

NINE-YEAR-OLD KARL van Beethoven remained with his mother at first, but a major struggle was about to begin. Beethoven refused to deal with his sister-in-law. He was anxious about Karl's education, and he was certain that he would be a better role model than Johanna in the child's life. Beethoven was determined to have his only nephew live with him. Johanna would not agree to such an arrangement, so her brother-in-law took her to court to try to settle the matter.

The first time Ludwig and Johanna appeared before a judge, it was decided that the pair would be joint guardians as had been requested in Caspar Carl's will. Beethoven was very unhappy with this ruling. In 1816 he returned to court to attempt to gain full guardianship of the child. Johanna had even appealed to the emperor, but her request was denied. The war over Karl continued for four years, with each side winning a few battles, until 1820 when Beethoven was finally awarded complete custody.

Learn About Sign Language

IN 1815 the American minister Thomas Hopkins Gallaudet began searching for a way to allow people who were deaf to better communicate in a hearing world. He traveled to Europe to study their methods of teaching youngsters with this handicap. Gallaudet met Roch-Ambroise Sicard, who was teaching at a school for the deaf in Paris. Sicard invited the American to learn their system. The French had developed a sign language that allowed their students to easily communicate by using their hands. Returning to America, Gallaudet founded the American School for the Deaf in Hartford, Connecticut. His sign language is used by countless people. If it had been available to Beethoven and his friends, the composer would have been able to converse without the use of conversation books.

You'll Need

∞ Sign language alphabet chart
∞ Internet access

1. Use the chart to practice the sign language alphabet until you are comfortable spelling out words.

2. Once you have mastered the alphabet, go on any of the websites that teach you common sign language phrases, such as www.lifeprint.com, the American Sign Language resource site.

3. Learn more about sign language and programs for the deaf and hard of hearing. Some suggested sites are:

∞ **Conference of Educational Administrators of Schools and Programs for the Deaf** www.ceasd.org

∞ **Laurent Clerc National Deaf Education Center at Gallaudet University** http://library.gallaudet.edu/Clerc_Center/Information_and_Resources/Info_to_Go/Resources/Websites_of_Schools_and_Programs_for_Deaf_Students_.html

∞ **National Association of the Deaf (NAD)** www.nad.org

4. There are programs that educate and assist people who are hard of hearing or deaf in most communities. Find out what is available in your school system or area; perhaps you can visit one of the programs.

American Sign Language chart Dreamstime

Karl was deeply disturbed by the ugly dispute between his mother and his uncle. He was now forced by the court to leave his mother's home and live with someone his mother clearly did not like. Beethoven called his nephew "dear Karl" and seemed to love him, but the composer had no real parenting experience, and his demanding personality created additional problems.

Disheartened and sad, Karl ran away from his uncle's house and back to his mother. He was quickly brought back to the home of his uncle, who then decided that it would be best to send the boy away to a boarding school. Again the youngster was required to adjust to a new situation. He had a hard time fitting in and did not do well at the school. When Beethoven was informed of the situation, he brought Karl back to Vienna, where he hired tutors for his nephew.

It was almost impossible for Beethoven to concentrate on anything else with all this turmoil in his life. The composer had normally worked on three or four compositions at once. He had told his friend Wegeler, "I never write a work continuously, without interruption. I am always working on several at the same time, taking up one, then another."

But now, for nearly two years following his brother's death, Beethoven did not compose much music. His mind was on his problems with Karl. He was constantly nervous, thinking about ways to handle the child and deal with the messy situation. At the same time Beethoven's hearing was deteriorating even further and his ear trumpets were not much help anymore.

Concerned with how to handle the problems he encountered with his nephew, Beethoven consulted his friend Nanette Streicher numerous times. She was a wise woman and a wonderful mother. They wrote many letters to each other, in which Beethoven regularly asked her advice about all sorts of things, and they also visited each other frequently. Nanette tried to help her friend but found that he was very stubborn, and although his love for his nephew was evident, she observed that Beethoven clearly had no clue about raising a child.

Although he was the boy's uncle, Beethoven wrote letters to Karl that usually addressed him as "My dear son" and ended with "your father." He forgave Karl many times and wanted very much to be close to him. One letter, written in 1825 after a disagreement between the two, unquestionably illustrates Beethoven's genuine fondness for his nephew.

My dear son,

Only nothing further—only come to my arms, you shall hear no harsh word. For Heaven's sake do not rush to destruction— you will be received as ever with affection— as to considering what is to be done in future, we will talk this over in a friendly way, no reproaches, on my word of honor.... Only come—come to the faithful heart of your father,

Beethoven

Most summers Beethoven left the sweltering city of Vienna for the cooler countryside. One place Beethoven enjoyed spending the warmer months was the medieval spa town of Baden. Located about 17 miles south of Vienna, the town with its warm baths and scenic surroundings

Beethoven's Letters

Throughout his life Beethoven wrote numerous letters to family members, friends, patrons, publishers, and the women he loved. These correspondences, along with his conversation books, have allowed future generations to have a richer understanding of the man. In these letters Beethoven wrote about his troubles, fears, frustrations, business dealings, financial problems, and personal relationships.

Many of Beethoven's letters to his publishers were about the difficulties he faced because there were no copyright laws. A publisher would buy the rights to a composer's works for a fee that they would negotiate. Once a piece was printed, some dishonest publishers would pirate the work to reprint it without permission and without paying the composer. It was extremely upsetting to Beethoven that these publishers not only stole his work but also often printed his music with errors.

Some of Beethoven's letters revealed his sense of humor, like a musical joke he sent to the **soprano** Anna Milder-Hauptmann in 1816 or witty melodies he mailed to his friend the Hungarian count Nikolaus Zmeskall. Now and then Beethoven would include a brief song or melody that he had composed for the receiver of the letter. Certain letters reveal his distrust, bitterness, and anger.

When he wrote to an admirer, Beethoven usually sent greetings to his or her family. His correspondence with Countess Erdödy, who had lost a child, was touching as he expressed the gentle and kind side of his personality. In these letters he asked the countess to embrace her remaining children, who, Beethoven stated, were dear to his heart. Often Beethoven ended his letters by asking the person to think of him and to remain his friend.

From a letter to Archduke Rudolph:

YOUR ROYAL HIGHNESS,—

I am better, and hope to have the honor of waiting on you in the course of a few days, when we must strive to make up for lost time. I always feel anxious and uneasy when I do not attend your Royal Highness as often or as assiduously as I wish. It is certainly the truth when I say that the loss is mine, but I trust I shall not soon again be so unwell. Be graciously pleased to remember me; the time may yet come when I shall be able to show you doubly and trebly that I deserve this more than ever.

I am your Royal Highness's devoted servant,

LUDWIG V. BEETHOVEN

attracted many wealthy Viennese. Several members of the Austrian royal family often spent their summers in the village. Baden is ringed by picturesque mountains and dotted with many lushly planted parks. This beautiful setting was the scene of a dreadful incident involving Karl.

For many years Karl had been upset over the continuous conflict between his mother and his uncle and frustrated with his own life. He loved to play billiards and had gambled away large sums of money. Karl was also disturbed by the fact that he never seemed to be able to achieve the goals his uncle had set for him and expected him to reach. He knew that his uncle had many big dreams for him as a musician or a scholar, but the young man did not study and had failed his examinations in school. How could he tell this to his uncle, who had hoped that his nephew would continue to attend the university?

His uncle had written to him, "You cannot honor the memory of your father better than to continue your studies with the greatest zeal, and strive to become an honest and excellent man." Karl felt even more pressure because his uncle had expressed the thought that Karl might be able to find a position as a college professor after he completed his studies. Karl realized that he was not able to make any of these dreams come

🎝 An antique postcard shows the houses Beethoven rented during his vacations.

true. Before coming up with this latest wish, his uncle had tried to steer him into a musical career. That had not worked out either, as Karl had little musical talent. Everything he had ever attempted to do just fell apart.

The young man looked at his options, and none of them seemed very good or even possible for him to attain. He felt so dissatisfied and down-hearted about his life—he had made so many bad choices and taken so many wrong turns. He determined that the solution to his problems was to end his life. On July 31, 1826, Karl hiked up to the remains of the Rauhenstein Castle perched on the top of a hill in Baden. The castle had been built in the 12th century and was a landmark in the town. When he spent summers in Baden, Beethoven had taken many of his walks among the ruins.

Climbing up the steep hill to the castle, Karl carried two pistols he had recently purchased. Luckily, he had no experience with guns and failed at his suicide attempt. The first bullet he fired missed; the second caused a head wound that was not fatal. When he was found, he cried out, "I went to the bad because my uncle wanted to better me." Karl was brought to his mother's home for a few days.

Since attempted suicide was a crime in Austria, he was taken from his mother's home and escorted to a hospital by the police. Karl was treated at the hospital for his head injury and questioned about

☙ Ruins of the Rauhenstein Castle in Baden. Reproduced with permission of the Ira F. Brilliant Center for Beethoven Studies, San José State University

why he would try to harm himself. The young man told the doctor that he was unhappy with his life and had to make changes. He explained that he had wished to join the military and be a soldier but his uncle was against the idea.

When he was released from the hospital, Karl wrote a heartfelt plea in his uncle's conversation book. He made it clear that he wished to be

Beethoven's Doctors

Throughout the years Beethoven had consulted many doctors about his multiple complaints and illnesses, including abdominal pain, depression, and wild mood swings, as well as his deafness. These men were distinguished physicians who treated many aristocratic patients. Unfortunately, medicine was not advanced enough to correctly diagnose and treat Beethoven's health problems.

His childhood friend Franz Wegeler did not personally treat the composer but advised him over the years. Wegeler suggested that Beethoven see Dr. Gerhard von Vering, the medical adviser to Emperor Joseph II, about his hearing loss.

Dr. Johann Frank was consulted from 1800 to 1809. He had served as the physician to the Russian tsar. He authored a nine-volume study of public health and made several clinical discoveries.

Giovanni von Malfatti tended to Beethoven from 1808 to 1816 until an argument ended their relationship. Ten years later, Dr. Malfatti was asked for help in treating the dying composer; he prescribed an alcoholic fruit punch as a remedy. Dr. Jakob von Staudenheimer advised taking the treatments at hot springs. He got irritated when Beethoven refused to follow many of his recommendations.

A professor at the University of Vienna, Dr. Anton Braunhofer treated the composer for six years, until 1826. This doctor prescribed a strict diet, which he recorded in a conversation book: no coffee, wine, or spicy foods. His stubborn patient refused to give up his wine. In 1826, Dr. Ignaz Wawruch took over and brought in the surgeon Dr. Johann Seibert to drain Beethoven's fluid-filled abdomen.

All of these doctors were respected for their knowledge and skill. They tried, with the limited medical information available to them, to bring relief to the composer. Beethoven was constantly concerned about his physical condition and discouraged that his health could not be restored.

permitted to enlist in the army. Beethoven was deeply troubled by this terrible event; he had always wanted to do what was best for his nephew. He realized how miserable Karl must have felt to consider ending his life. The army would provide

⚜ Baron Joseph von Stutterheim.

100

Karl with direction and discipline. Beethoven decided to finally approve of Karl's desire to enlist in the army and began to assist him in accomplishing his goal.

The composer contacted several of his friends who might be able to help Karl receive a military assignment. It turned out that his old friend Stephan von Breuning had the right connections and would make the arrangements. Karl was told to report to a regiment of the Austrian army under the command of Baron Joseph von Stutterheim, the lieutenant field marshal, in the middle of December. Beethoven dedicated his String Quartet in C-sharp Minor (op. 131) to Baron von Stutterheim in gratitude for accepting Karl into his regiment.

Seeing how ill his uncle had become, Karl delayed reporting to his regiment until January 2, 1827. Meanwhile, they started to search for a doctor who could cure or at least ease Beethoven's many ailments. Dr. Andreas Ignaz Wawruch, a member of the Imperial Medical Society, agreed to examine Beethoven and try to find the appropriate treatments. Arriving to examine the composer, the doctor wrote in Beethoven's conversation book, "One who greatly reveres your name will do everything possible to give you speedy relief."

10

REACHING THE HEIGHTS

*"Music should strike fire from the heart of man,
and bring tears from the eyes of a woman."*
—LUDWIG VAN BEETHOVEN

EVEN WHILE BEETHOVEN was dealing with personal troubles and ailments, he was writing some of his finest pieces. His "late period" began around 1815, about the same time that his brother passed away. His sketchbooks are filled with ideas for new works at that time, though his compositional output declined until the guardianship of his nephew was settled by the courts.

By 1820 Beethoven was back to his normal routine of rising early, carefully counting out the number of beans to grind for the pot of coffee that was his breakfast, and then working on a composition or two until mid-afternoon. Now his compositions became

✿ Crowds gathered for Beethoven's funeral.
Beethoven Museum, Bonn

even more original, unconventional, and intense. These later works noticeably demonstrate Beethoven's genius.

Beethoven's Ninth

ONE OF Beethoven's most-loved works, his Symphony no. 9 in D Minor (op. 125), is called the *Choral* Symphony. It is the final complete symphony that Beethoven wrote, and he was the first major composer to use voices in a symphony. Beethoven started working on the symphony in 1818; it took him almost seven years to complete. The result would become the best-known symphony in classical music. The Ninth Symphony is considered his symphonic masterpiece.

Writing music was never an easy process for the composer, and this particular work was going to take a great deal of planning and effort. Beethoven drew out over 200 musical sketches for his choral symphony. He made many attempts to find the right musical mixture to ensure that the movements of the symphony worked well together and tried many different combinations to find the exact blend that suited what he wanted the notes to communicate to listeners. Beethoven had always believed in freedom, justice, and equality, and now he wanted to write these convictions about universal brotherhood into his music. Once the first three movements

took form, the composer decided that he needed to find an ending for this symphony that would impart these ideals.

For 30 years he had wanted to put the famous German poet Johann Christoph Friedrich von Schiller's poem "Ode to Joy" to music. Its words cried out to Beethoven for the correct notes to express them. Always bold and inventive with his music, he felt that the poem would be the perfect vehicle for the conclusion of this symphony. Knowing that a finale sung by a chorus had never been used in a symphony before, Beethoven worried about how it would be accepted if he dared to try it. And he was not sure that it would work.

The symphony was already quite long with the three movements that had been written, longer than any other symphony yet composed. Beethoven wondered, how would a choral fourth movement be tied into an already lengthy work that began with three instrumental movements? His uncertainties made him write a completely different instrumental alternative (which he later employed in a different piece) to the choral movement. But the composer kept returning to the idea that Schiller's poem would be absolutely perfect for a fourth and final movement and finally concluded he would use it.

His decision made, Beethoven still needed to figure out which of the verses to include. He continued to give it a great deal of thought and tried out many sketches. None of them seemed to work

✶ Johann Christoph Friedrich von Schiller.
Courtesy of Marcus Kaar, portrait.kaar.at

well enough. Then one day, while a friend was visiting, Beethoven looked up from his sketchbook and exclaimed, "I have it! I have it!" The concept of how to use the poetry fell into place as he furiously penned the notes onto the paper.

Using Schiller's verses as a guide, the composer outlined a score. He just needed a few more lines to open the poem. Beethoven added these words of his own to the introduction: "O friends, not these sounds! Rather, let us sing something more pleasant, more full of gladness." Next the chorus would perform the first three verses of Schiller's ode. Beethoven included only one-third of the original poem and arranged the verses in an order that made sense to him. A chorus followed each of the eight stanzas. The total movement proclaimed that all people should live in joy and friendship. Beethoven gradually created his message to humanity.

The symphony, commissioned by the London Philharmonic, was supposed to debut in London. In a twist of fate it was first performed in Vienna in 1824. Beethoven was now 54, and it was his first public concert in a decade. The score noticeably stated that it had been dedicated to Friedrich Wilhelm III, the king of Prussia, without mentioning the London Philharmonic. The following year, when the work was finally performed in England, the printed manuscript made it clear that the symphony had been composed for the Philharmonic Society in London.

"Ode to Joy"

The Enlightenment era emphasized the ideal of tolerance for all people and the concept of universal brotherhood. Enlightenment thinkers believed that reason would lead to harmony and social justice for all mankind.

Johann Christoph Friedrich von Schiller (1759–1805) was one of Germany's leading literary figures. His writings were celebrated for their **lyrical** style and moral vision. Schiller believed that people could look past their differences and come together in friendship. His poem "An die Freude" (Ode to Joy) was written in 1785. It reflected his deep belief in equality and unity among all people and freedom and liberty of the individual. Historians explain that Schiller had first entitled the poem "Ode to Freedom" but that the royal censors had required that the poet replace the word "freedom."

"Ode to Joy" appealed to many composers. It was set to music the same year it was published, and within a short time more than a dozen composers used it as the text for their songs. Beethoven considered setting it to music as early as 1793. In the final chorus of *Fidelio* he included a line from the poem, "Whoever has won a lovely woman, join in with our jubilation!"

Schiller's ode celebrates human possibilities; it stresses friendship and peace. Beethoven adapted Schiller's poem to suit the last movement of his Ninth Symphony, but Schiller's original words still shine through the changes. Both men shared the same vision, and through Beethoven's music, Schiller's poetry reached the minds and hearts of millions of people.

A Great Concert

WHILE WORKING on the Ninth Symphony, Beethoven also was composing the Missa Solemnis in D Major (op. 123). The Latin name means "solemn mass"; a mass is a ritual act of worship in a church. The composer had spent more than one year researching church music before he began working on this piece. Beethoven had been asked to write the music for this mass by his patron, friend, and student Archduke Rudolph,

Archduke Rudolph (1788–1831)

Rudolph von Habsburg-Lothringen was the brother of Francis, the Holy Roman emperor of Austria, and was one of Beethoven's most important patrons. He was the youngest of 15 children born to Emperor Leopold II and Maria Luisa, the daughter of the king of Spain. His early education focused on many academic areas, but he most enjoyed his music lessons, which led him to discover that he had talent. His excellent piano performances were highly regarded in the salons of Vienna. Around 1803 he began to study piano and composition with Beethoven. These lessons continued until 1824, sometimes on a daily basis. The men wrote to each other frequently; the archduke saved more than 100 of these letters.

In 1805 Rudolph was preparing for a military career, but his bouts of epilepsy and his religious feelings caused him to change

course. Although his life was devoted to the church, his interest in music continued. In his 20s, however, arthritis in his hands ruined his ability to play the piano. For many years the archduke paid Beethoven a yearly salary and frequently helped him with other expenses. In gratitude Beethoven dedicated 14 of his works to him. In 1820 Rudolph von Habsburg-Lothringen was appointed as the archbishop of Olmütz, a city in the Austrian empire.

An avid collector of manuscipts and books, the archduke's library contained many first editions of Beethoven's scores. Rudolph's own compositions included a trio for clarinet, cello, and piano; a sonata for piano and violin; and 14 Variations on a Theme by Ludwig van Beethoven. The archduke died in the spa town of Baden at the age of 43.

for performance during his installation as an archbishop. Archduke Rudolph had been a great supporter and financial backer of the composer for many years, and Beethoven saw granting his request as a way to express his appreciation for his patron's generosity and goodwill.

In 1819, outlining his objectives for the music, Beethoven had written to the archduke, "The day on which a High Mass composed by me will be performed during the ceremonies solemnized for Your Imperial Highness will be the most glorious day of my life, and God will enlighten me so that my poor talents may contribute to the glorification of that solemn day." He added, "My chief aim when I was composing this grand mass was to awaken and permanently instill religious feelings, not only in the singers, but also in the listeners."

Often feeling unwell, Beethoven was falling behind in his composition of the work. He recognized that the mass was not going to be completed in time for the scheduled March 1820 ceremony. It took the composer four and a half years to complete the Missa Solemnis. As usual, he toiled over other compositions at the same time, often putting the mass aside for a while.

Beethoven was earnestly religious but not a man who attended church services. Born a Catholic, he practiced little of its ritual and formal observances, yet his library was full of spiritual books including the Bible, Kant's *Theory of the*

Heavens, Plutarch's writings, Shakespeare's plays, and the works of Goethe and Schiller. In his draft of the Missa Solemnis score Beethoven wrote, "To my God, who has never abandoned me."

When he finally finished composing the Missa Solemnis, Beethoven realized that it would be a challenge for both the singers and the instrumentalists. Since the mass took almost 90 minutes to

Create Liner Notes for a Beethoven CD

THE TRADITION of album notes began when the backs of vinyl record sleeves displayed printed information about the recording. With compact discs, or CDs, "liner notes" providing information about the music or the musicians are inserted into the CD cases. Music scholar Richard Osborne wrote the liner notes for a collection of Beethoven's symphonies played by the Berlin Philharmonic and conducted by Herbert von Karajan. Osborne comments on each of the symphonies. His statement about the Sixth Symphony includes the detail that Beethoven once refused to rent rooms in a house that had no trees around it. He includes in the liner notes Beethoven's quote, "I love a tree more than a man," which sums up the composer's feeling about nature. Write your own liner notes that would make someone want to listen to the music.

You'll Need

∞ Your favorite Beethoven work, such as a symphony or a sonata
∞ Music-listening device (such as an iPod, computer, or CD player)
∞ Internet access
∞ Pen and paper
∞ Computer with word-processing program
∞ Scissors
∞ CD case (empty)
∞ Glue or tape (optional)

1. While listening to your favorite Beethoven work on your iPod, computer, or CD player, jot down notes about the following on a piece of paper or type them up on your computer.

∞ The title of the piece you have selected
∞ The name of the composer
∞ The name(s) of the soloist(s) (if performing with an orchestra) or the performer(s)
∞ The name of the orchestra
∞ The name of the conductor

2. Describe something about the music or the musicians performing the piece. You might want to read other liner notes on the Internet to research information about the performers, the orchestra, and the conductor.

3. What insight can you give the listener about this work? Can you relate a story about the composer that you've learned in this book to this selection of his music? What makes this recording special?

4. Open up a blank document on your computer and set the margins to form a 5-by-4½-inch rectangle. Now type up your notes to fit into the rectangle. Print out the page, cut the rectangle out, and fit it into the CD case. Or, if you are using the same Beethoven work you designed a CD cover for, you could glue or tape the notes to the back of that CD cover.

perform, he also grasped that it was probably too long for a church service. The work was to premiere in St. Petersburg but presented such difficulties that a December performance, which was intended to benefit musicians' widows, could not take place. The debut of the entire piece was held off for four months, until April. Beethoven inscribed the manuscript with the words "From the heart … may it go to the heart."

Once the arrangements for the concert were made, there were only three days left to rehearse. The Ninth Symphony and an overture plus three movements from the Missa Solemnis were scheduled to be performed at the same time. All of the pieces proved difficult and demanding. The concert tickets were sold out—every seat was taken. After the performance, at a dinner celebrating the success of the concert, Beethoven accused the producers of cheating him when they claimed they had earned only a small profit due to the high cost of the production. The angry composer stormed out of the party.

The first three parts of the Missa Solemnis had been introduced along with the Ninth Symphony in Vienna on May 7, 1824, in the Kärntnertortheater. This symphony required the largest orchestra that had ever been gathered for a work. The composer had further increased the size by adding two musicians instead of one for each wind instrument. The Ninth Symphony was an explosion of emotion that struck the audience with great force. Beethoven sat on the stage facing the orchestra and the conductor. After the performance the audience went wild with applause that he could not hear. One of the singers came over to him and turned the composer around to face the audience so that he could witness their wonderful appreciation of his work. Beethoven was intensely touched by their response.

A Visit to the Countryside

AT THIS time of his great musical success, Beethoven was coping with his nephew Karl's suicide attempt and coming to terms with his decision to join the army. Karl had left the hospital but still needed to rest and recover fully before he was well enough to report to his regiment. Beethoven himself had not been well, but under the care of Dr. Wawruch he was beginning to feel better. His brother Nikolaus Johann had asked Beethoven to come to his country estate in Gneixendorf for a visit. Beethoven decided that this would be a good place for his nephew to relax and gather his strength. They left Vienna on September 28, 1826, arriving in Gneixendorf the next day.

The village in which the pharmacist Nikolaus Johann and his wife lived was about 60 miles north of Vienna. The scenic countryside always inspired the composer, and while he was visiting his brother's home he took long walks, composing in his head, humming, and conducting the air. The people of Gneixendorf were surprised by his odd behavior and sloppy appearance, just as the inhabitants of Heiligenstadt had been puzzled and amused so many years earlier. Beethoven tried not to notice their stares as he often paused his stroll to pull one of his notebooks out of a pocket to write down an idea.

While visiting Gneixendorf, Beethoven composed a string quartet and began to work on other compositions. Some days were very

Composers Influenced by Beethoven

Composing over a 35-year period, Beethoven always strove for perfection, laboring over each note. He was a great innovator who expanded the limits established by previous composers. He set high standards for other composers to follow.

Franz Schubert (1797–1828) tried to avoid having Beethoven's music influence his compositions, but he was a strong admirer of the man. He dared to experiment with traditional musical forms just as Beethoven had done. He also lived in Vienna and visited Beethoven during his last days. Schubert once complained, "Who can do anything more after Beethoven?"

Beethoven influenced the music of the Romantic composer Robert Schumann (1810–1856), who wrote much of his lyrical music in the classical forms. Schumann's Second Symphony, in tribute to Beethoven, employs a "fate" theme, has an extended **coda**, and develops an expanded scherzo. Schumann recognized Beethoven as a genius and embraced the standards he had set.

Franz Liszt (1811–1886), a composer and piano virtuoso, idolized Beethoven. Liszt is known as the creator of the **symphonic poem**, a one-movement orchestral piece that evokes imagery. Musicologists believe that he may have used Beethoven's *Pastoral* Symphony as his inspiration for this type of program music.

Johannes Brahms (1833–1897) was another Romantic composer who was dedicated to the classical forms. He composed so much in the spirit of Beethoven that a conductor called his First Symphony "Beethoven's Tenth." Brahms continued the traditions of the Classical era.

Gustav Mahler (1860–1911) was the last Viennese symphonic composer in the line stretching from Beethoven. His intense, massive, and aggressive music often requires an expanded orchestra. Four of his symphonies use a chorus or a solo voice. Mahler crafted his works with the same attention to detail that Beethoven had employed.

Even modern "pop" and experimental musicians have included some of Beethoven's greatest compositions in their works. An example is Walter Murphy and the Big Apple Band's "A Fifth of Beethoven," a disco dance tune based on the Fifth Symphony. Beethoven's symphonies have also been used in many feature films such as *Fantasia* (Sixth Symphony), *Die Hard* (Ninth Symphony), and *Mr. Holland's Opus* (Seventh Symphony).

Discover How Your Lungs Work

WHEN BEETHOVEN contracted pneumonia he found it difficult to breathe because of fluid in his lungs. When you breathe, air passes down the windpipe to the lungs in your chest. Beneath the lungs is the diaphragm, a dome-shaped muscle whose movements alter the air pressure in the lungs, allowing them to take in and release air. Using balloons, you can see how lungs inflate when you inhale air and contract when you exhale.

Adult supervision required

You'll Need

∞ Utility knife

∞ 1-liter clear plastic bottle (a water or a soda bottle, rinsed well, will work)

∞ Scissors

∞ Large balloon

∞ 2 rubber bands

∞ Straw

∞ Small balloon

∞ Modeling clay

1. With adult assistance, carefully use the utility knife to cut off the bottom of the plastic bottle.

2. Cut the neck off the large balloon with the scissors.

3. Stretch the balloon over the bottom of the bottle.

4. Place a rubber band around the balloon to hold it in place. This balloon acts like your diaphragm.

5. Insert the straw into the small balloon, keeping it in place with a rubber band.

6. Place the small balloon into the mouth of the bottle so that the straw is sticking out and the balloon is inside the bottle but not touching the larger balloon on the bottom. This smaller balloon represents your lungs.

7. Use the modeling clay to secure the straw out of the top of the bottle. Make certain that the straw stays open so that air can pass through.

8. Hold the bottle in one hand while gently pulling down on the balloon stretched across the bottom of the bottle. What is happening? When you inhale, the diaphragm moves downward while other muscles attached to the ribs pull the ribs outward. This causes the chest cavity to expand, allowing a vacuum that draws air into the lungs.

9. Release the bottom balloon. What is happening? When you exhale, the diaphragm and rib muscles relax and air moves out of the lungs.

stressful since the brothers often did not get along. Too frequently, old quarrels were brought up and rehashed without being resolved. New arguments seemed to arise unexpectedly as well. The trip had originally been planned as a brief stay, but Beethoven and his nephew had been there two months. Since Beethoven was not feeling well, he decided to return to his own house and doctors in Vienna. As the frost of winter approached, the composer was certain that they had remained away from home for too long. He made the arrangements to leave as November ended and December began.

Embarking for Vienna on a cold and rainy day, Beethoven climbed into an uncovered carriage. Soon after Beethoven arrived at home it was obvious that he was very sick, shaking and burning with a fever. On the journey he had contracted pneumonia, which was filling his lungs with fluid. Each breath was painfully labored; he was urged to go to bed, but Beethoven stubbornly insisted that "there are things to look after and work to complete."

Beethoven had been working on a new symphony and wanted to continue to compose. But feeling so sick, he found it hard to concentrate. His lungs hurt every time he took a breath, and he alternately roasted from the fever and then suddenly began to tremble and shake. Beethoven pushed himself to work, knowing that he still had much to do, much to accomplish. He had once told a friend, "I feel as if I had written scarcely more than a few notes."

Finale

BY MARCH, Beethoven could not leave his bed, and his doctor was again summoned. He complained of stomach pains and could barely speak. Coughs interrupted every few words. The doctor drained fluid out of his stomach and put a poultice on the wound. He did all that he could to help his patient recover.

Karl, who had finally reported for duty in January, came for a visit and could see that his uncle was very sick. Before returning to his military regiment he wrote a note saying that he would soon come again. But Karl was not certain that his uncle would live even a few more days and was not sure he could see him alive when he returned. Once his nephew departed, Beethoven realized that he had something important to do—he had to make his final arrangements. Beethoven signed his will leaving everything he had to his nephew.

Beethoven's friends, sensing that the end was near, gathered around his bedside keeping a vigil. The mood was gloomy both inside the house and outside. Dark clouds gathered in the March sky while a harsh wind blew through the still-bare branches of the trees.

Late on the afternoon of March 26, 1827, there was a startling thunderstorm. Booming claps of thunder and dramatic flashes of lightning were causing fireworks to appear in the heavens. The sudden beams of light flickered outside the window, occasionally highlighting the bed in which Beethoven lay in a coma. Suddenly a peal of thunder erupted and Beethoven opened his eyes, raised his body, and lifted his right arm with his fist clenched before sinking back onto the bed. Just then the people assembled in the room realized that Beethoven had died.

❧ *Beethoven's Dream*, an engraving after the painting by Aimé de Lemud. Library of Congress LC-USZ62-85831aa

More friends came to keep watch by his bedside until the funeral would take place. One of the visitors was Gerhard, the 12-year-old son of Stephan von Breuning, who had come to see his father's friend often during the last two years of Beethoven's life. Beethoven had moved to an apartment located just around the corner from his lifelong friend in a building named Schwarzspanierhaus (meaning "the house of the black-robed Spaniards"—the structure had once housed a monastery for Spanish monks). The youngster hung onto the composer's every word and paid so much attention to him that Beethoven gave the boy the nickname "Trouser Button," meaning that Gerhard kept as close to him as a button on his pants. Beethoven had enjoyed these visits and having the companionship of someone so much younger and amusing.

Gerhard had been very observant of everything surrounding his musical idol. Years later he wrote a book describing what he saw and heard during the last few years of Beethoven's life entitled *Memories of Beethoven: From the House of the Black-Robed Spaniards*. In this book Gerhard talked about his familiarity with Beethoven:

The friendship that grew out of our living so near to each other—a renewed friendship from younger days for my parents, a new friendship for me—was to be as short an episode in my young life as it was inspiring, and it was to end

so unexpectedly and painfully as to remain in my memory for as long as I live. It might be that the brevity of the episode even heightened the impression on the happy and carefree twelve-year-old I then was. Though the stroke of fate that ended the period changed my life utterly, my memories of that happy time shall remain with me forever.

Gerhard described that he and his father, Stephan von Breuning, had gone to Beethoven's apartment the day after Beethoven's death. Wanting to obtain a memento of the man they had both respected and loved, they had the intention of cutting off a lock of his hair. Walking into the room where Beethoven was lying in his casket, they discovered that others must have had the same idea before their arrival. There were no more locks of hair left to take. Gerhard was heartsick realizing that he would have to forgo having this keepsake of a man he had so admired, but it made him realize how many people had loved the composer and had also wanted a special reminder of his life.

On Thursday, March 29, only three days after Beethoven's death, the March sky was blue and the sun was shining. All of Vienna was in mourning; even the schools had been ordered to close for the day. Soldiers were stationed on the streets to assist the police assigned to direct and control the thousands of people who had come to Beethoven's funeral.

The Chronicle of Beethoven's Hair

A recent book by Russell Martin and Lydia Nibley, titled *The Mysteries of Beethoven's Hair*, tells the amazing story of how a lock of hair that was clipped from Beethoven's head arrived in America. In the 18th century it was an accepted practice to keep a bit of hair as a reminder of someone dearly loved. Several friends of the composer had snipped off pieces of Beethoven's famous hair right after he died.

One particular lock, cut off the day after Beethoven's death by Ferdinand Hiller, a 15-year-old musician who had visited the ill composer a number of times, took an amazing journey through history. Hiller later became a composer and conductor. He placed Beethoven's hair in a small frame made of glass and wood. Hiller treasured this memento and in 1883 presented it to his son Paul. The hair was passed to each succeeding generation of the Hiller family, who finally took it with them as they fled Nazi Germany during the Holocaust to what they hoped would be greater safety for Jews in Denmark.

During World War II the keepsake was given to a doctor who helped save Jewish lives. It came to an auction house in 1994, almost 50 years after the Second World War ended, where two American admirers of Beethoven purchased it. Ferdinand Hiller had handwritten a description of what was contained inside the small frame and attached the note to its back. Some of the strands were taken out to be DNA tested, but most of the hair was left in its glass container, which is on display at the Beethoven center at San José State University.

An estimated 20,000 admirers, including many well-known artists, had gathered near Beethoven's house. His plain oak casket had been placed on a table in the courtyard, and a wreath of white roses was draped over the coffin. A throng of people rushed into the open space in front of the Schwarzspanierhaus. So many people tried to come close to the coffin that the soldiers had to push them back through the courtyard gates.

Ceremonial music was played before the coffin was lifted by the eight men serving as pallbearers, including Beethoven's friend and former pupil Carl Czerny and the composer Franz Schubert. They solemnly carried the casket from the courtyard of the Schwarzspanierhaus. Surrounded by musicians carrying candles, the pallbearers slowly stepped down the street lined with thousands of people on the way to the parish church on Alserstrasse.

Following the casket were Beethoven's brother Nikolaus Johann, his nephew Karl, and Stephan von Breuning with his son Gerhard. Because of the crowd, it took over an hour to reach the church, which was only one block away. The musicians played Beethoven's "Funeral March" from his Piano Sonata no. 12 (op. 26).

During the church service the soldiers tried to keep the masses of people under control—so

❦ Stephan von Breuning. Courtesy of Marcus Kaar, portrait.kaar.at

❦ RIGHT :Some 20,000 people gathered for Beethoven's funeral. Beethoven Museum, Bonn

many were crying or upset. At the conclusion of the service large groups on horseback and countless carriages followed the horse-drawn hearse to the Währing Cemetery in northwestern Vienna. Several of the coaches in the procession belonged to the royal family. It was an impressive funeral that paid tribute to a great artist.

The Währing Cemetery was not to be Beethoven's final resting place. In 1888 his remains were moved to the Zentralfriedhof, Vienna's largest cemetery. A magnificent monument marks his grave.

Austria's leading playwright Franz Grillparzer had written a eulogy that was read by Beethoven's friend the actor Heinrich Anschütz. This tribute spoke for all the people attending the funeral and all who admired Beethoven's work. Grillparzer's words said, "He was an artist, and who can stand beside him? Like the behemoth storming through the seas, he rushed on to the limits of his art . . . so he was, so he died, and so he will live for all time."

❦ Beethoven's grave monument in Vienna.
Photograph by Daderot

115

ACKNOWLEDGMENTS

THANK YOU TO the entire staff at the Chicago Review Press, especially Lisa Reardon, the developmental editor. Special thanks to my grandchildren, Julia and Jean, for testing the activities. I truly appreciate the proficiency of Susan Silberman, who diligently worked on the musical examples. Over the years it has become apparent to me that without the assistance of my husband I would not be well informed about the myriad functions and immeasurable potential of a computer; I extend my gratitude to him for bringing my technical skills into the 21st century. I also must acknowledge my former music teachers who instilled a love, understanding, and appreciation of classical music in me and so many others.

Resources

Recommended Recordings, DVDs, and Websites

Recordings

Arthur Rubinstein: Beethoven Piano Sonatas **(RCA)**

This is a remastered recording of works by Arthur Rubinstein, one of the greatest pianists of the 20th century and a wonderful interpreter of Beethoven's music. Included on this CD are:

- Piano Sonata no. 8 in C Minor (*Pathétique*), op. 13
- Piano Sonata no. 14 in C-sharp Minor (*Moonlight*), op. 27/2
- Piano Sonata no. 23 in F Minor (*Appassionata*), op. 57
- Piano Sonata no. 26 in E-flat Major (*Les adieux*), op. 81a

Beethoven: Greatest Hits **(RCA)**

This CD offers a good sampling of Beethoven's works. The orchestras, conductors, and soloists performing on the CD are celebrated for their excellence. An enjoyable choice for starting a Beethoven collection.

Beethoven: The 9 Symphonies (Deutsche Grammophon)

Featuring Leonard Bernstein conducting the Vienna Philharmonic Orchestra, this set of all nine symphonies is outstanding. The music was recorded during magnificent live concerts.

Beethoven: The Piano Concertos (Decca)

The Israel Philharmonic Orchestra is conducted by Zubin Mehta in this boxed set featuring the Romanian pianist Radu Lupu. The orchestra and soloist interact flawlessly on this CD. The recordings were made over a 20-year period and put together for this collection.

Beethoven's Wig: Sing Along Symphonies (Rounder Records)

Crazy lyrics are set to pieces of music by various great composers in this CD, which has been nominated several times for Grammy Awards as best musical album for children. The songs provide information about the composers as well as their fabulous music. You can sing or dance along with these funny songs and then listen to the music without the lyrics.

DVDs

Beethoven Lives Upstairs (Devine Videoworks Production, 1992; directed by David Devine)

This TV special tells a story about a boy who lives in a building where Beethoven is a tenant. It features excerpts of Beethoven's best-loved works conducted by Walter Babiak. (Also available as a book.)

In Search of Beethoven (Microcinema, 2010; directed by Phil Grabsky)

This documentary investigates the composer's life. Grabsky interviewed historians and musicians across America and Europe for the film. The narration is complemented by various musicians performing parts of Beethoven's works.

Places to Visit, in Person or Online

Immerse yourself in Beethoven's world by visiting these sites either online or, if you have the opportunity, in person!

The American Beethoven Society

http://americanbeethovensociety.org

An international organization devoted to the study and appreciation of Beethoven's life and music. The society publishes the biannual *Beethoven Journal* and sponsors many events throughout the year including concerts, lectures, dinners, film screenings, and the Annual Young Pianist's Beethoven Competition.

Beethoven-Haus Museum

www.beethoven-haus-bonn.de

Bonngasse 18-26

Bonn, Germany

The museum is located in the house in which Beethoven was born. Housing the largest collection of Beethoven memorabilia in the world, the museum also contains a digital archive offering virtual exhibitions of the composer's life and recordings of his works.

Beethoven the Immortal

www.lucare.com/immortal

This site dedicated to the life and work of Beethoven includes excerpts of Beethoven's letters, images, audio downloads, and more.

The Ira F. Brilliant Center for Beethoven Studies

www.sjsu.edu/beethoven

The Beethoven Center is located in Room 580 in the special collections area on the fifth floor of the Dr. Martin Luther King Jr. Library. The King Library is on the campus of San José State University at 150 E. San Fernando Street, San José, California. The Guevara Lock of Beethoven's hair is on display. The center's collections include many manuscripts and scores, historical keyboards, paintings, and other objects relating to the composer.

Ludwig van Beethoven's Website

www.lvbeethoven.com

This website has a great deal of information about Beethoven. It includes contributions from Beethoven admirers from many countries presented in an interesting manner.

Mad About Beethoven

www.madaboutbeethoven.com

Another website dedicated to the composer containing lots of information and facts about his life. The site is hosted by a British journalist and Beethoven enthusiast who has written books and consulted on various projects regarding the composer.

GLOSSARY

accent the emphasis on a beat so that it is louder or longer than another in a measure

accompaniment the support provided through harmony, rhythm, or melody to the main theme in a piece of music

aria a song performed by a single voice

arpeggio a broken chord with the notes sounded separately

Baroque era the music of the period from 1600 to 1750

cantata a sacred or secular text set to music and sung with instrumental accompaniment; includes several movements, solos, duets, and choruses

chamber concerts music intended for a smaller group using a limited number of instruments

Classical era the music of the period from 1750 to 1830

clavichord an early keyboard instrument

coda conclusion

concerto (plural: concerti or concertos) a musical composition in which the interest is focused on a solo performance

counterpoint combines two separate musical lines or melodies that interact at the same time

crescendo growing louder

debut a first appearance or performance; a premiere

duet a composition for two musicians

dynamics the loudness or softness of a composition

embellishment ornaments added to music to make it more interesting

ensemble a musical performing group such as a chorus, orchestra, or chamber group

finale final; the last movement of a piece of work

flat a sign that lowers the pitch of a note (♭)

fortepiano the type of piano built in the 18th century; predecessor of the piano

genre describes the standard category or style of a work

Gregorian chant a melodic line without harmony used in early church music

harmony the sounding of two or more tones simultaneously

harpsichord stringed, keyboard instrument; the strings were plucked by quills

improvisation music created by the musician during a performance

Kapellmeister (German) a director of music for a court or chapel

key a specific series of notes that have a particular tonality

libretto the text of an opera or oratorio

lyrical having the form and musical quality of a song

manuscript a document containing the notes of a composition

measure contains a specific amount of musical time; created by the notes written in the space between the bar lines

melody tones of different pitches arranged together to form a pattern

minuet a graceful French dance

motif a melodic/rhythmic unit that is a major building block of a work and is often repeated throughout a piece of music

movement a complete, self-contained section within a larger musical work

nocturne an instrumental piece that is short, lyrical, and free in form

notation how music is expressed in writing

note a sound of specific and distinct pitch, quality, and duration; also called "tone"

octave a group of eight tones arranged in a pattern of steps

opera a play that is sung; contains costumes, scenery, and acting

opus a classification of compositions to show their chronological order; from the Italian for "work"

oratorio a play (usually on a religious subject) that is sung without the costumes, scenery, and acting of an opera

orchestration the art of writing a score for the orchestra

ornamentation the decoration of a melodic line to add interest (example: adding a trill, which alternates between two tones)

overture an introduction; from the French *ouverture*, meaning "opening"

pitch the highness or lowness of a tone

premiere a first performance; a debut

program music instrumental music which conveys a mood, tells a story, or illustrates a picture

quartet a composition calling for four instruments

range the lowest to the highest note in a piece of music, or that is possible for the human voice or an instrument to reach

Renaissance era the music from the period of 1450 to 1600

rhythm the combination of long and short, even and uneven sounds that communicate a sense of movement

Romantic era the music from the period of around 1800 to 1900

scherzo (plural: scherzi) the Italian word for "joke"; in ¾ time and in three-part form

score the pages depicting all of the instruments and voices in a composition

sharp a sign that raises the pitch of a note (♯)

sonata a large instrumental work containing a cycle of contrasting movements

soprano the highest female voice

staff the framework upon which the notes are written

symphony a large musical work for an orchestra; from the Greek *sumphónia* meaning "harmonious"

symphonic poem a piece of program music for orchestra in one movement that evokes imagery; also called "tone poem"

tempo the speed of the rhythm in a composition

theme the subject; a musical passage that states an idea

tone a sound of specific and distinct pitch, quality, and duration; also called "note"

trio a composition calling for three instruments

variation a change in the theme that makes it different but still recognizable

virtuoso a skilled performer

volume the degree of loudness or softness with which a musical piece is to be played

waltz a three-beat dance with the accent on the first beat: ONE, two, three, ONE, two, three . . .

BIBLIOGRAPHY

Books marked with an asterisk (∞) are suitable for kids ages nine and older.

Bagar, Robert, and Louis Biancolli. *The Concert Companion*. New York: McGraw-Hill Company, Inc., 1947.

Beethoven, Ludwig van. *Beethoven's Letters*. Edited by Arthur Eaglefield. New York: Dover Publications, 1972.

Beethoven, Ludwig van. *Beethoven: The Man and the Artist as Revealed in His Own Words*. Edited by Friedrich Kerst and Henry Edward Krehbiel. The Project Gutenberg EBook, 2002.

Burney, Charles. *A General History of Music*. New York: Dover Publications, 1957.

Comini, Alessandra. *The Changing Image of Beethoven: A Study in Myth Making*. New York: Rizzoli, 1987.

Forbes, Elliot, ed. *Thayer's Life of Beethoven, Part I*. New Jersey: Princeton University Press, 1991.

Forbes, Elliot, ed. *Thayer's Life of Beethoven, Part II*. New Jersey: Princeton University Press, 1967.

Grout, Donald Jay. *A History of Western Music*. New York: W. W. Norton, 1973.

Lockwood, Louis. *Beethoven: The Music and the Life*. New York: W. W. Norton, 2005.

Marek, George. *Beethoven: Biography of a Genius.* New York: Funk and Wagnalls, 1970.

∞ Martin, Russell, and Lydia Nibley, *The Mysteries of Beethoven's Hair.* Watertown, MA: Charlesbridge Publishing, 2009.

Morris, Edmund. *Beethoven: The Universal Composer.* New York: Harper Collins, 2005.

Pfeiffer, Carl. *The Art and Practice of Western Medicine in the Early Nineteenth Century.* Jefferson, NC: McFarland, 1985.

Schindler, Anton Felix. *Beethoven as I Knew Him.* New York: W. W. Norton, 1996.

Schonberg, Harold C. *The Lives of the Great Composers.* New York: W. W. Norton, 1997.

Schulenberg, David, ed. *Music of the Baroque: An Anthology of Scores.* New York: Oxford University Press, 2001.

Shedlock, John South. *Beethoven.* London: George Bell and Sons, 1903.

Solomon, Maynard. *Beethoven.* New York: Schirmer Books, 2001.

∞ Von Breuning, Gerhard. *Memories of Beethoven: From the House of the Black-Robed Spaniards.* Cambridge: Cambridge University Press, 1992.

Music Dictionaries

Kennedy, Michael, and Joyce Bourne, eds. *The Concise Oxford Dictionary of Music.* London: Oxford University Press, 1996.

Sadie, Stanley, and Alison Latham. *The Grove Concise Dictionary of Music.* London: Macmillan, 1994.

Sadie, Stanley, and John Tyrrell. *The New Grove Dictionary of Music and Musicians.* London: Macmillan, 2000.

Slonimsky, Nicolas. *Baker's Biographical Dictionary of Musicians.* New York: Schirmer Books, 2001.

Index

Page numbers in *italics* refer to pictures.

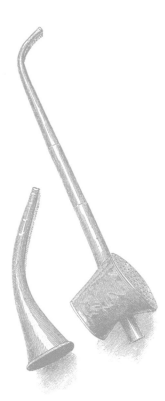

Chicago Review Press celebrates the arts with these other fine titles in the "for Kids" series

American Folk Art for Kids

With 21 Activities
By Richard Panchyk
Paper, 9781556524998
$16.95 (CAN $ 25.95)

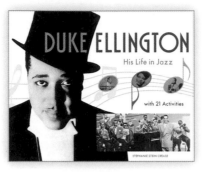

Duke Ellington

His Life in Jazz with
21 Activities
By Stephanie Stein Crease
Paper, 9781556527241
$16.95 (CAN $18.95)

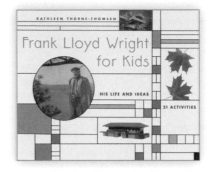

Frank Lloyd Wright for Kids

His Life and Ideas,
21 Activities
By Kathleen Thorne-Thomsen
Paper, 9781556522079
$16.95 (CAN $25.95)

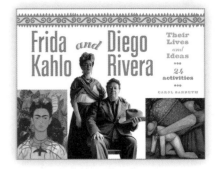

Frida Kahlo and Diego Rivera

Their Lives and Ideas,
24 Activities
By Carol Sabbeth
Paper, 9781556525698
$17.95 (CAN $25.95)

Leonardo da Vinci for Kids

His Life and Ideas,
21 Activities
By Janis Herbert
Paper, 9781556522987
$17.95 (CAN $19.95)

Monet and the Impressionists for Kids

Their Lives and Ideas,
21 Activities
By Carol Sabbeth
Paper, 9781556523977
$17.95 (CAN $26.95)

Salvador Dalí and the Surrealists

Their Lives and Ideas,
21 Activities
By Michael Elsohn Ross
Paper, 9781556524790
$17.95 (CAN $26.95)

Van Gogh and the Post-Impressionists for Kids

Their Lives and Ideas,
21 Activities
By Carol Sabbeth
Paper, 9781569762752
$17.95 (CAN $19.95)

Available at your favorite bookstore, (800) 888-4741, or www.chicagoreviewpress.com

CHICAGO REVIEW PRESS

Distributed by IPG
www.ipgbook.com

www.chicagoreviewpress.com